Nick Derutter

CAREER IN SCUBA

How to Become a Dive Instructor and be Successful

First edition: September 2020
Second edition: January 2024

ISBN 979-8-35094-630-7

DiveSAGA
Pumpkin Hill, Utila 34201
Honduras, Central America
www.divesaga.com/media

WWW.DIVESAGA.COM

"The impossible missions are the only ones which succeed"

Jacques Yves Cousteau

CAREER IN SCUBA
How to Become a Dive Instructor and be Successful

Introduction by the author

Get Prepared

1. 7 Habits of a Successful Dive Instructor
2. Getting Your Life Sorted
3. Training Agencies, Dive Centers and Equipment
4. Setting Expectations

Get Started

5. Writing a Good Scuba Resume and Social Media
6. How to Land Your Dream Job
7. Common Mistakes on the Job
8. When Things Go Wrong

Get Better

9. Safeguard Your Future – Visa, Insurance and Retirement
10. Finding Your Niche
11. Becoming an Industry Leader
12. The 20% Club

13. Advice and Stories from the Pros

Appendix

Introduction

Hi there! You are about to read the second edition of my book 'Career in SCUBA - How to become a diving instructor and be successful'. I'm extremely grateful for your trust in this resource and I hope it will live up to your expectations.

"If you want to make a million dollars in SCUBA diving, you better start with two million and lose one" is the famous saying when people share their plans to enter the diving industry as a professional. With this book, I am hoping to make a case for the industry as a whole and for diving professionals in particular. It will show you that with thorough preparation and the right attitude, you will be able to turn this dream into a real career.

You may not make a million dollars along the way (although that's really up to you and your drive and creativity and I certainly know people who did it) but you will find out that there are a variety of options to grow your career, earn a decent and steady income and still live the lifestyle that is so often the reason people choose this career path.

The fact that this book is now having a second edition, further proves the point that anything SCUBA related has commercial viability, so long as it is a quality product with a heart and a soul. Whether it be your SCUBA classes, diving trips, innovative diving equipment or in fact this book, people are willing to spend on quality diving experiences.

Still, the choice to become a full-time SCUBA instructor is not an obvious one and leading this lifestyle will require you to break away from the traditional concepts of what a 'career' is. There is no SCUBA University (unless maybe some dive centers who go by that name) and there is very little industry regulation and standardization beyond what the training agencies and local communities have put together. Building a successful career for yourself in this industry will require dedication and love for the sport and the motivation to make your own way, doing something you love while getting paid for it.

Although this book is not necessarily about me, it is worth noting that I have personally always worked and lived by the principles that are described in this manual. In just a few years, I have found myself in the position of a successful and very happy SCUBA instructor trainer, having certified over 3000 divers in disciplines ranging from Open Water Diver to Trimix Instructor and SCUBA Instructor to Underwater Photographer. Besides running Instructor training programs at well established dive centers in the Americas and Europe, I also own Dive SAGA, an online dive business with a webshop, dive travel and an online diving magazine. (www.divesaga.com)

You may also want to have a look at my 'Dive SAGA' YouTube channel and Instagram page to stay in the loop.

I acknowledge that "success" can be measured in many different ways and isn't necessarily the same for everyone. For the purpose of this book (and my personal life) I define "success" as a state of emotional and financial balance and well-being while having the freedom to pursue your passions.

There are only a few things in life that have given me the same sense of fulfillment that I get from seeing people become divers, and even more so from seeing divers become dive professionals. It is my hope that this document will be a fast-pass through some of the mental, motivational and administrative obstacles that many of us have had to overcome when becoming a diving professional.

GET
PREPARED

1. The 7 Habits of a Successful Dive Instructor

In Stephen Covey's best seller "The 7 Habits of Highly Effective People" the author lays out a framework for seven very simple rules to live by if you want to succeed in your field. Let's jump into this book and our career in SCUBA by immediately adopting a "career mindset" and let's sculpt our own principles to live by, going forward.

PREPARATION

The entire first act of this book is about preparation, and really, there's no way around it. If you're going to turn your life around and add a fantastic new credential to your resume, you will need to get your ducks in a row.

Make a check-list and write down what you need to accomplish in order to make a career as a dive instructor happen. Will you work in your home country or abroad? Full time or part time? Do you have back-up finances?

For those of you who are planning to teach SCUBA as a full time job (more about that later), you will really need to take it one step at a time, earn the necessary credentials, gain experience and think about what sort of life you would like for yourself.

Preparation will be an ongoing theme in your life as a dive instructor. Every student you teach will need your undivided attention, which means you won't have the time, nor will you need the distraction of having to figure out logistics on the spot. This means you'll need to make it a strong habit to prepare your classes from A to Z before they start. After all, you will be taking direct responsibility over people's lives.

The secret sauce for most successful diving activities (training, expedition or otherwise) is always preparation through thorough analysis, planning and communication.

DEDICATION

For most people, the only way to become successful in something is to be really good at it. If you're good at something, people with similar interests will find you and pay you for whatever that is that you do. The only way to become truly good at something is of course to be really into it.

Perhaps you've heard of the 80/20 Principle by Richard Koch. In his book "The 80/20 rule", he states that it takes only 20% of the effort to be just as good as 80% of the people in your field. It is the extra 80% of effort, of true, relentless dedication that will make you belong in the top 20% super-performers of your area of expertise. In this case, SCUBA instruction.

 An often quoted statistic is that 80% of diving instructors don't renew their teaching credential after just two years in the industry. While that may seem a scary number at first, it's really only a problematic statistic if you are aspiring to belong to the 80% who quit. If you can muster up the dedication to belong to the 20% who make it past the two-year mark, you're in a very exclusive and well-connected club.

It's no secret that many people take the plunge to become a dive instructor and that not everyone succeeds. It will be your dedication that will truly set you apart. Keep improving yourself, work hard every day, read, learn and develop a "Yes I can!" attitude.

Rather than spreading yourself thin over five different skills, pick one and stick with it. If dive instruction is for you and you stick with it, you'll be able to turn yourself into a truly remarkable industry leader.

DETERMINATION

Let's be straightforward here: this is not an obvious career choice and you're going to get some quizzical looks when you tell people about your project. Living the life of a SCUBA instructor is the dream of many but the reality of only a few.

Many people around me were absolutely convinced I would be long sold into slave trade with, at best, a kidney missing before I would ever be able to support myself financially as a dive instructor. It's true that a little bit of determination is needed. There's more underpaid jobs than jobs with decent pay, and twelve to fourteen hour days are not unusual in the industry, but who cares? If this is your passion and you're really going for it, you'll have a blast.

Later on, we'll talk about finding a job position that's right for you but it's very possible that along the way, you may find yourself in spots that don't seem to be working out. Don't give up easily. One of the problems with the diving industry is that the market is frequently flooded with new professionals and they're of course easy hires for employers looking to pay minimum wage for mediocre performance. It takes time to gain experience and to set yourself apart from the crowd.

Most who enter the recreational diving industry as a "professional" will do so as an experiment. They're looking for a gap year experience or maybe even for an excuse to escape the traditional labor market with no real intention of working hard. I will say this many times throughout this book: treat it as a real career and it will be!

PATIENCE

It would not be hard to fill a whole second book with stories about patience. As a dive instructor you're going to need patience and a lot of it! It's a 'people' job, and having a passion for the peace and quiet of the ocean alone just won't cut it. You'll be dealing with people who are afraid, people who are over enthusiastic and also people who, despite their best efforts, just don't get it.

Ask any old school military style instructor and they'll tell you that diving is not for everyone. It's only for the lucky few who are fit, fearless and committed. While a certain level of fitness and commitment is obviously required to learn this beautiful sport, the truth is that with enough patience and practice, many people can learn how to dive safely. Everyone who can be turned into a safe, confident and competent diver is a potential return customer for the future and if you did it right, you will be the one who they turn to when looking for additional training; more than likely because you believed in them and got them to where they wanted to be.

Be patient, allow people to progress at their own pace, and work hard to ensure that you always keep a smile on your face while doing so!

FLEXIBILITY

If you're looking for regular hours and a clearly laid out career path, you should probably ask for a refund on this book. (Just kidding, you won't get one)

The diving industry, wherever you go, can be chaotic. Everyone has their own story about how they made it and you'll soon discover that no one got there the same way. There's no standardized income and in certain locations around the world labor laws may not really apply, let alone a minimum wage. In some areas around the world competition may be strong and you'll really need some flexibility to get the job.

I'm not telling you to forget your ambitions and work for peanuts, not at all. Work with what you can get and slowly craft your career the way you want it out of the options that cross your path. Try to get along with everyone, try to learn from people, and try to make connections. You'll find that the professional diving community is small. Flexible, reliable people are the ones who tend to get the opportunities.

SAFETY

If you're following the guidelines in this book, you'll be working hard with all your heart to build a wonderful career in diving. You'll be overcoming some hardships, coming up with new ideas and getting people excited about diving. Eventually, you will have crafted the life for yourself that you have always wanted to live. As I always tell my instructor candidates: After all that hard work, don't let ANYONE ever take that away from you.

Despite the joyful and enticing advertising images of divers exploring the oceans, SCUBA diving is dangerous and it's of the utmost importance to never forget that. You are becoming a dive professional and your job is to mitigate that danger. Any time human beings go underwater, there is a risk of drowning. Any time human beings breathe compressed gas, there is a risk of decompression sickness and lung overexpansion injuries.

It takes a split second of distraction, a moment of poor planning or a perfect storm of unforeseeable circumstances to put you in the undesirable spotlight of litigation. You are the diving professional, the highest in rank and the one who's ultimately responsible for the safety of everyone you supervise. All it takes is a single lawsuit to strip you of your job, your teaching credential and a whole lot of money.

We will be talking about professional liability insurance in chapter seven, and during your instructor course your trainer will take you through the proper steps of risk management. Though what you need to take away from this manual is that a successful diving instructor always puts safety above anything else. Fun, adventure and a decent profit margin are all essential ingredients to a healthy diving business, but they will always come second to safety.

ENTREPRENEURSHIP

It's a common argument among skeptics that there's no money to be made in diving, that the market is saturated, the economy is down and the natural environment is in decline.

 When Barry Coleman started diving in the 1970's I'm sure he didn't exactly know what he was getting into. However by the early 2000 he had designed his own first rebreather and not long after he would establish an entirely new training agency, called RAID (more about RAID later) because he didn't think other training agencies at the time catered to rebreathers the way he thought they should.

This is a great example of entrepreneurship. Diving is such a multi faceted industry and there are many more ways to produce an income than just teaching diving. It's important to realize this, because keeping an open mind to opportunities within the industry is what may make or break your "survivability" as a diving professional.

All in all, diving as a sport (and as a business) is not that old. Recreational diving really only started in the sixties and even then, it didn't really kick off on a large scale until the eighties or nineties. This means that there is still a lot of room for innovation and new ideas.

Did You Know?

At the time of writing, the deepest ever SCUBA dive was to a depth of 332.35m / 1,090 ft 4.5 in by Egyptian Special Forces Officer Ahmed Gabr. The descent alone took 12 minutes.

2. Getting Your Life Sorted

2.1. Teaching SCUBA as a Side Job at Home

For many, diving is a hobby and even when moving on to the professional levels they choose to keep it that way. Just like SCUBA diving for recreational purposes, teaching SCUBA can be a hobby too. For some divers, this is what keeps them diving. The ability to teach others and introduce them to the excitement and wonder of the underwater world can be a great way to stay involved in diving in your local area, even if the local dive sites have little new secrets for you.

Many people still prefer to take a few weeks off of work, travel to a tropical area and pursue their instructor training there. The reason for this is that the weather often allows for a full-time training schedule and the influx of recreational courses on a daily basis allow for a more immersive experience, rather than completing the instructor training course over several months during the weekends. Other people prefer to tackle their instructor training at a local dive center and go the slow route. There's something to be said for taking your instructor training in the area where you plan on teaching but it's not essential, as long as you are proficient at the local diving techniques.

If you have a daytime job that is too good to give up, but you would still like to become a diving instructor, this book can certainly put you on the right track to help you choose a training center, think about ways to market yourself and grow your career.

Depending on what sort of arrangements you can make with your local dive center, you may teach with them during evenings and weekends. You may choose to become a freelancer or independent instructor and source your own students in your immediate area. Many dive training agencies allow for this way of teaching and dive shop affiliation is not always required (but often recommended because they can provide you with more customer leads and peer support).

You won't need to make too many immediate lifestyle changes if you're only planning to teach part time, and the step to becoming a dive instructor is also not an overly expensive one. It could simply be a great addition to your skills set. Take some time off work, become a SCUBA instructor and see what works in your area.

2.2. Teaching SCUBA as a Full Time Job at Home

Depending on where you live, there may be a very vibrant SCUBA diving market in place, or diving may not be popular at all. If you're looking to make a full time career out of teaching SCUBA in your home town and you're going all in, you may need to do a bit more research because expectation management is everything. While setting up a new market can be very challenging and you may need to surround yourself with some experienced people, it's not impossible.

Whatever environment you are in, if you have decided to teach SCUBA diving at home and you're expecting it to be profitable, you'll probably need to do some research. Ask yourself (and find answers to) the following questions:

- How competitive is my local area?
- If there is plenty of competition, how will I offer something different?
- Will I work with someone established in the area or set up my own business?
- If there is no competition, why are there no dive centers in my local area?
- Is the local population interested in SCUBA diving?
- If so, why aren't they diving right now?
- Does the local population have sufficient disposable income?
- What other activities do people spend their disposable income on in the area?
- How is SCUBA diving perceived in my area?

It may seem challenging at first to get your hands on this type of information but a simple survey with your immediate circle of acquaintances may be a great starting point. Websites like www.surveymonkey.com are free and easy to use to gather the most immediately needed information to analyze your local market. This information should give you a better idea of the potential in your area. Usually, training agencies are also able to help their members with up-to-date business statistics for their local area and if you're trying to establish a new market, they may be very keen on lending a helping hand.

Keep in mind that, even if there are already some local dive operators active in the area, that doesn't mean you can't offer something new. Plenty of places in the United States, for instance, had a very active diving population but failed to acquire new, younger divers, resulting in a shrinking of the local diving industry. Sometimes all the diving industry needs in a certain location is some fresh ideas and motivation. That could be you!

That being said, if you plan on making SCUBA instruction in your local area a full time job, it will be crucial to make a thorough cost analysis and fully understand what you'll need to charge for your courses and activities. If local competition is present, a price comparison could be a good idea but don't get hung up on what others charge. Your expenses and profit margins may be very different from theirs and ultimately these will determine your prices.

SWOT ANALYSIS

If you are planning to start your own business or already know you'll be trying to tap into a new or unusual market, a good way to figure out if your plan is viable is to complete the analysis below.

A SWOT analysis is a strategic planning technique often used by businesses or individuals to help identify the strengths, weaknesses, opportunities and threats to a specific project.

Don't forget: With some creative thinking, weaknesses and threats are just opportunities, waiting to be discovered!

SWOT MATRIX	HELPFUL TO THE OBJECTIVE	HARMFUL TO THE OBJECTIVE
INTERNAL ORIGIN	STRENGTHS	WEAKNESSES
EXTERNAL ORIGIN	OPPORTUNITIES	THREATS

2.3. Teaching SCUBA Abroad

Of the many instructor candidates that come through our training centers, the majority have made the decision to work as a dive instructor as a way to fund a simpler, more adventurous lifestyle abroad, away from the corporate hustle and bustle of their home countries. For many people, teaching SCUBA is the ticket to freedom.

I would fall into this category as well. Although I live in Central America and am now a resident of the republic of Honduras, I left Belgium years ago to pursue a life in which travel, adventure and international encounters stood central. Despite being frowned upon and often discouraged by many, I haven't regretted this decision once and I would encourage everyone to make that same move, if this is what your heart tells you to do.

There are a few extra considerations to teaching SCUBA abroad, such as the need for added social security and an effective system to save money for the future. Many of these considerations will be dealt with in chapter 7 'Safeguard Your Future', but it is necessary to address some of the concerns that you probably already have, if teaching abroad is part of your plans.

When I left home, I already knew where I would take my training, had gathered a decent kit of diving equipment, bought insurance (also see chapter 7) and had some extra money saved up beyond what would be needed during training. This was to ensure that I would be able to support myself for a few more months while looking for that first job. Besides that, all I had was a one-way ticket and an open mind.

People will tell you it's unrealistic to leave your home country with no job set up. Personally, I told them it's probably even more unrealistic to spend tens or even hundreds of thousands of Dollars on a university degree with equally as little guarantee of employment. Job security doesn't usually happen before you obtain a degree in any industry, and diving is no different. So relax, you'll get there.

When teaching abroad there are many options, ranging from somewhat seasonal work in the European and North-African

Mediterranean, to year-round jobs in the Caribbean and South East Asia. Whether you prefer seasonal or permanent employment is really up to you and your plan. Many dive centers love to hire short term staff for six to eight months so they don't need to deal with underpaid, bored staff when low season hits. Other areas around the world have a more consistent influx of divers and may prefer instructors to commit for a year or even multiple years.

It's also not unusual for people to have two or more skills that allow them to alternate, such as teaching SCUBA during the summer months in let's say Mexico, and then relocate north to Canada to work as a ski or snowboard instructor. (But again, keep in mind, it's my recommendation that you focus on doing one thing really well first)

When it comes to organizing your international lifestyle, the only limit is the one you set for yourself. There are lots of job opportunities going around and it's up to you to be the right person for the job. Whatever you do, don't let people convince you that it's impossible. Sure, it's not "normal", but if normal was what you wanted, then you probably wouldn't be reading this book.

SCUBA TOURISM HOTSPOTS

Did You Know?

NASA prepares astronauts for complex weightless space tasks in their 'Neutral Buoyancy Laboratory', a giant pool in Houston, Texas.

3. Training Agencies, Dive Centers and Equipment

3.1. Training Agencies

At this point you may or may not realize that individual dive centers or instructors don't write their own curriculum (although they could if they wanted to). Most reputable SCUBA training worldwide is conducted through one or more training agencies. These are for-profit or non-for-profit (generally private) organizations whose business model or mission statement is to design dive courses and issue certification credentials.

Instructors and dive schools often associate with one or more training organizations through which they offer training. Their choice for a particular training organization is usually based on which agency is favored by local divers or what the market demands. Dive centers and dive instructors then pay a licensing fee, to obtain the rights to use the agency's methodology and materials. You may recognize this concept as a version of a franchise.

We'll look at a list of the most common training agencies in a bit but first, let's understand that the individual agencies also follow a set of rules for their training and all have a similar course flow that is dictated by the International Standard Organization (ISO). The general training scheme usually looks like this:

- Experience Programs: A supervised try-dive during which participants can safely try diving, without committing to a course. These experience programs don't yield a certification but may credit towards future training.

- Entry Level Certification: Largely revolves around the diver learning HOW to dive independently (with a buddy) and how to safely use SCUBA equipment. This level is often divided into a supervised entry level and an autonomous entry level.

- Advanced Diver Certification: Divers learn awareness of their dive environment, as well as how to execute tasks underwater beyond their personal diving skills.

- Rescue Diver Certification: Divers learn the techniques and philosophies behind looking after other divers' safety and what to do in the most common emergencies. A CPR/First Aid credential is usually needed in order to partake in this level of training and many agencies will offer their own version of a CPR/First Aid credential.

- Dive Guide Certification: Divers learn how to plan and supervise dives and guide other certified divers on tours. This is usually the first professional level of certification.

- Dive Instructor Certification: The diver learns how to use the agency's curriculum to teach beginner and advanced level diving courses to individuals.

- Special activities and Decompression Certifications: Most agencies also have a long list of specialized activities such as enriched air or wreck diving, to name a few and a series of courses that teach decompression diving techniques, which involve considerably more hazards than recreational diving. Chapter 8 talks more in depth about these activities.

A more extensive list of the specific certifications available through the most popular training agencies is available in the appendix at the end of this book.

At the risk of getting technical, if you're curious what the general European and International Standards Organization's requirements are for each level, here's a little summary (if not, just skip a page)

- *EN 14153-1/ISO 24801-1 Recreational diving services -* Safety related minimum competence requirements for the training of recreational scuba divers - Part 1: The level 1 "Supervised diver" has sufficient knowledge, skill and experience to dive, in open water, to a recommended maximum depth of 12 m, which do not require in-water decompression stops, under the direct supervision of a dive leader, in groups of up to four level 1 scuba divers per dive leader provided the dive leader is capable of establishing physical contact with all level 1 scuba divers at any point during the dive, only when appropriate support is available at the surface, and under conditions that are equal or better than the conditions where they were trained.

- *EN 14153-2/ ISO 24801-2 Recreational diving services -* Safety related minimum competence requirements for the training of recreational scuba divers - Part 2: The level 2 "Autonomous diver" has sufficient knowledge, skill and experience to make dives, in open water, which do not require in-water decompression stops, to a recommended maximum depth of 20 m with other scuba divers of the same level, only when appropriate support is available at the surface, and under conditions that are equal or better than the conditions where they were trained without supervision of a scuba instructor, unless they have additional training or are accompanied by a dive leader.

- *EN 14153-3/ ISO 24801-3 Recreational diving services -* Safety related minimum competence requirements for the training of recreational scuba divers - Part 3: The level 3 "Dive leader" has sufficient knowledge, skill and experience to plan, organize and conduct their dives and lead other recreational scuba divers in open water. They are also competent to conduct any specialized recreational scuba diving activities for which they have received appropriate training, and to plan and execute emergency procedures appropriate for those diving environments and activities. If diving and environmental conditions are significantly different from those previously experienced, a level 3 "Dive Leader" requires an appropriate orientation with regard to local environmental conditions, and may require appropriate specialized training and experience to lead dives which have more demanding operational parameters.

- *EN 14413-1/ ISO 24802-1 Recreational Diving Services -* Safety related minimum requirements for the training of scuba instructors - Part 1: A level 1 scuba instructor is competent to teach and assess scuba students up to level 1 on their theoretical knowledge and skills in confined water. If supervised and authorized by a level 2 instructor, also to gain experience in teaching and assessing the theoretical knowledge of scuba diver levels 2 to 3, teach any level of scuba diver in confined water, and gain experience in teaching and assessing open water surface skills, and if directly observed and supervised by a level 2 instructor, to gain experience in teaching and evaluating any skills in confined and open water.

- *EN 14413-2/ ISO 24802-2 Recreational Diving Services -* Safety related minimum requirements for the training of scuba instructors - Part 2: A level 2 scuba instructor is competent to plan, organize and conduct dives and lead other recreational scuba divers of all levels in open water, including rescue activities, teach and assess students up to scuba diver level 1, 2 and 3, to supervise level 1 scuba instructors, and to plan, organize and conduct scuba diver training courses. With suitable additional training or experience the level 2 instructor is competent to plan, organize and conduct speciality training and diving operational activities.

If a training agency wants to produce a curriculum that can stand its ground on the international market, they have to follow these standards. As a result, if an individual dive instructor or a dive school wants to have any relevance in today's diving industry, they will associate with a training agency that follows these standards too.

Of course, the intention of this book is not to persuade you towards any one training agency. There are perfectly good reasons for choosing any of the agencies below, as well as others on the market. There are over 50 training agencies worldwide and we can't possibly cover them all. This chapter is simply intended to make you consider the differences and how this choice may affect your later career.

Listed below are some of the biggest and most globally represented agencies. One thing you need to understand is that they are very similar in their set-up. All offer multiple certification levels, all have theory, confined water and open water segments and almost all comply with ISO standards.

Keep in mind that a choice for a training agency is rarely an exclusive one and far less of a big deal than you may think. Many successful instructors around the world carry more than one agency's teaching credential to increase their employability and customer service options.

Most agencies also offer 'instructor crossover training', which allows you to learn the specifics of the agency you're aspiring to cross over to, without having to learn how to teach all over again.

Lastly, the agency you take your instructor training with does not have to be the same agency as the one that issued your initial recreational diver certifications. Up until the level of Divemaster, Dive Control Specialist or any other 'dive guide' certification (names differ from one organization to another) it is usually very easy to enroll in classes with another agency without need for a crossover course.

MARKET SHARE PER TRAINING AGENCY

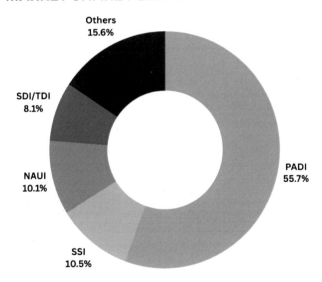

It's very hard to come by reliable data on SCUBA training agency market share. The above graph is based on numbers produced by divebuddy.com in 2018, according to their members' agency affiliation. These numbers change all the time, but at least this will give you a sense of market share. Of course there are dozens of training agencies but for simplicity reasons, they are grouped under "others".

Let's have a look at some key information about some agencies.

PADI – The Professional Association of Diving Instructors (www.padi.com)

- PADI is by far the agency with the largest market share, represented in over 180 countries and territories across the globe which creates plenty of opportunities for new PADI Open Water Scuba Instructors.
- PADI certifies the vast majority of diving instructors and the credential doesn't necessarily set you apart from the others unless you're willing to specialize.
- PADI Instructors don't need to be affiliated with a dive center or resort. While this is the preferred method for teaching courses, independent instructors can teach courses up to Divemaster, as long as they use the appropriate system and materials.

Slogan: "The Way the World Learns to Dive"

NAUI - National Association of Underwater Instructors (www.naui.org)

- NAUI, founded in the United States in 1959, is the oldest diver training agency and is a non-profit organization.
- The NAUI ICC (Instructor Certification Course) became the first course to make diver certification available worldwide and internationally.
- NAUI has some high profile members, starting with Jacques-Yves Cousteau all the way to Kevin Costner and Cameron Diaz and likes to advertise this fact.

Slogan: "Diver Safety Through Education".

SSI - Scuba Schools International (www.divessi.com)

- Founded in 1970, a key difference with most other agencies is that SSI instructors can only teach courses through an SSI dive center.

- A very broad range of continuing education courses and "XR - Extended Range" Technical courses.

Slogan: "Comfort Through Repetition"

TDI/SDI - Technical Diving International / Scuba Diving International (www.tdisdi.com)

- Originated in 1994 as TDI with a focus on technical diving. SDI is a sister company which offers recreational courses. For ease of understanding, we have grouped them together in this chapter.
- TDI says it offers the broadest range of technical courses available on the market.
- Active in over 100 countries
- Particularly known for their sport-level 'solo diver' course.

CMAS - World Confederation of Underwater Activities (www.cmas.org)

- Not a training agency by itself but rather an international organization that recognizes local training federations. A complete list of these federations can be found here: http://www.cmas.org/federation-list
- Though often locally very strongly represented and respected, an instructor certification from a federation in one country is often not immediately recognizable elsewhere.
- Members generally support a more militaristic approach to diver training.
- In the case of CMAS it's important to understand that they don't issue the certification but rather recognize the following levels, as issued by their member agencies.

RAID - Rebreather Association of International Divers (www.diveraid.com)

- A very young but up and coming dive training organization which was founded in 2007 to support diver training for the Poseidon Mk VI Discovery Rebreather.
- It has since extended its scope to include open circuit scuba training and training for both recreational and technical diving sectors as well as snorkeling and freediving.
- RAID claims to have the most advanced training model in the industry today, with over 60 programs online and a 'no classroom' approach.

3.2. "Free Instructor Internship Courses"

I receive emails on a daily basis from people who are looking for 'free internships' or 'work experience' opportunities. There's nothing wrong with that and I answer every inquiry with the same enthusiasm, but in my case the answer is 'no'. While working experience is very important, it has nothing to do with receiving free training.

By now you've read a few times that many people in the diving industry seem to think there's no money to be made. My advice is to surround yourself with people who think otherwise. If you're taking free training in exchange for some free labour, you're inadvertently learning from someone who doesn't believe in receiving proper pay in exchange for decent instruction or hard work. I would dare to argue that this is the completely wrong first step to a successful career because it immediately locks you into the 'free' or 'cheap' mindset (but many will disagree with me).

I can't say I've ever really worked a day for free but I also can confidently say that I have always given my work my full 200% dedication. If you've ever seen 'The Dark Knight', you probably remember the Joker saying: "If you're good at something, never do it for free". I suggest you start taking that advice to heart (although that's probably the only advice you should ever take from the Joker).

The diving industry has been growing exponentially for the last 50 years and tourism is the only industry that didn't shrink during the financial crisis of 2008, although it did of course get hurt during the covid-19 crisis of 2020. People are willing to put down some decent cash for a priceless and safe diving experience, and so should you. A good instructor trainer will probably have built up a solid reputation and because of that, people will be willing to pay them for their expertise. Ask yourself: why should I want to learn from somebody who doesn't need to get paid for their efforts? Will someone put in the same time and effort if they aren't getting paid? Why are they depending on free labor to accomplish work around their dive center? There's always a catch, so don't take the bait.

If you treat your certification like a cereal box diploma, that's what you'll get out of it too. Surround yourself with people who have turned their careers into a success. Chances are, they will know how to help you achieve the same. When people pay me for their instructor training course, I always guarantee that my time and expertise will extend after the training as well. When writing a CV or looking for a new job position, I am always willing to help. In fact, I'm happy to do so because the candidate has paid me an honest fee, out of respect for my hard work, so that respect is mutual.

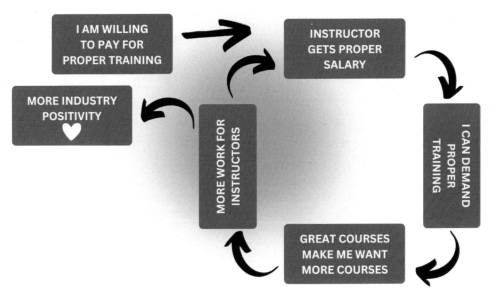

3.3. Who Do You Want To Be?

Every training center will have their own philosophy. While the curriculum is pretty much set in stone by the training agency, there can be a vastly different approach in how this curriculum is delivered (if it is even delivered in full at all).

At the dive centers I've partnered with, we decided on working with small groups only and extending the average duration of classes. While this initially seemingly limits our income potential, it actually increases the individual time spent with each student. As a result of this, our instructors are able to make a much better report with their divers and talk more about continuing education, therefore students tend to stay around much longer and take more courses.

During our instructor training we decided to add an entire workshop dedicated to dive center management, resume building and one where we allow candidates to sample new equipment such as full face masks, technical gear, as well as trying out sidemount gear. As a result of that, our candidates tend to follow the same teaching philosophy later in life. Essentially, we're leading by example.

Unfortunately, it can be very easy to fall into a trap of teaching mediocre courses, big groups, vague instruction, cutting corners. The problem with this is that it inevitably starts chipping away at your own industry longevity. Research shows that customers are seven times more likely to spread the word on a negative experience, as opposed to a good one. Overcrowded courses, bad work or a sloppy reputation will eventually catch up with you because, as we mentioned earlier, the productive population of the industry only consists of about 20% of the people, and they talk.

It speaks for itself that there are different philosophies and none of them are necessarily superior to the others, but during your research for a training center of your preference, think about who you want to be as an instructor and if the center's philosophy matches your own.

3.4. Dive Equipment

Let's put some thought into owning your own SCUBA kit. Depending on who you ask, people will tell you that you should own a full set before even becoming a Rescue diver or a Divemaster, while others may suggest you better wait a little until you really know what you want. So what are the pros and cons?

PRO

- A big plus side to owning your own set of diving equipment before you embark on your professional journey is that you'll be comfortable during training and you'll learn your equipment inside and out before it's time to teach others. This will greatly improve your trim, positioning and comfort levels in the water and also remove some of the stressors that come with being in a training situation.

- A second benefit to owning your own gear prior to your professional training is that most employers expect instructors to own their own equipment, which means that you'll be instantly hireable if you already do. It's one less expense to worry about afterwards, if you spend it before training.

CON

- While you may understand what dive equipment you like as a certified diver, being a dive instructor is a whole different game when it comes to the requirements that you will have for your kit. As a recreational diver, I really enjoyed my ultra light back inflate BCD. I had perfect trim and it was streamlined and compact for traveling. When I started teaching, however, I got increasingly annoyed with the lack of big pockets to store all my training aids and this became a big frustration. Now, I actually prefer the bulkier wrap-around style jacket with big pockets with zippers and a lot of metal D-rings. Priorities change when you start teaching.

- Secondly, the months spent as a Divemaster and Instructor in training are probably some of the more dive-intense and social times of your life, and you'll be meeting a lot of other divers. This will allow you to try out different pieces of equipment, which is a big benefit. After all, no retailer would let you take a BCD for a dive before buying it but your peers just might!

- A third argument for not immediately purchasing all of your diving equipment before training is that some dive centers expect their employees to wear the shop's brand. Let's say the dive center you end up working for is a Scubapro dealership and sources a big chunk of their revenue from equipment sales, then chances are that they will want you to wear Scubapro gear on the job.

In conclusion, if you already own your own set of diving equipment, you'll find a way to make it work and it will allow you to enter the job market much more quickly. If you don't own your own kit, maybe hold off on buying one but incorporate it in your budget as an expense that you will make anyway. Try out different things during your training and buy what you like from a teaching perspective.

Some items you will need anyway are a risk-free investment, such as a surface marker buoy, a compass, a dive watch/timer, a dive knife or underwater cutting device, a whistle and perhaps a basic dive computer.

If you're planning on working abroad and you're not sure where you'll end up, a solid piece of advice may be to choose brands that are globally available. This ensures that, in case something breaks, you'll have customer support and servicing options available wherever you are.

Did You Know?

SCUBA is an acronym that stands for Self Contained
Underwater Breathing Apparatus

4. Setting Expectations

4.1. What It Isn't

Do you dream of endless summer days on the beach? Sipping cocktails with your students while you explain some basic SCUBA stuff? Walk home tipsy at the end of the day and count your money in bed with the sand still between your toes?

Yeah me too but that's probably not going to happen.

As deeply as some people seem to believe in the misconception that there is absolutely no money to be made, others seem to be equally as delusional that this whole career choice is a walk in the park (or rather, on the beach). The truth is, both assumptions are extremes that might exist but neither one is a very realistic proposition for building a successful career.

Perhaps the image of the easy going SCUBA instructor who spends their days on the beach free of worry stems from misguided attempts at playful (or deceiving?) advertising. Perhaps it stems from people who only enjoyed a rather short (and probably not very lucrative) stint in the industry. Whatever the reason, a viable career in SCUBA probably involves a little bit less carefree beach time than you may think, and a little bit more get-to-business time than you may want.

It is of course okay to want to spend some time in a carefree way, and find the resolution to that desire on some long forgotten beach on some long forgotten island. There is nothing wrong with craving an escapist experience like this, but what you just imagined is indeed a vacation.

Teaching SCUBA is not a vacation. Even though many of your friends and relatives may eventually develop the impression that most of your life is one protracted vacation, the truth is that it will probably be anything but that. SCUBA diving is hard, physical work. Lifting SCUBA cylinders day in, day out can be taxing. Giving your students the personal and emotional attention they desire can be mentally exhausting. Ensuring your class's safety in the water can be challenging and demanding.

If I just burst your bubble, I do apologize. However, it's probably for the best. Teaching diving is an amazing occupation and I enjoy it almost every day. Very few of those days are spent actually bumming around on a beach though.

It is not rare that potential instructor candidates conduct their first conversation with me under the impression that they too have found life's ultimate hidden cheat code: become an instructor and never work a day in their lives! I'm sorry to be such a party pooper my friend.. the burger in the photo does not look like the burger that will land on your plate, I'm afraid.

4.2. What It Is

So what is it then? You don't have to have a million dollars in the bank to start a career in SCUBA but it's also not a chill life under the palm trees? Correct.

The longer my career in diving becomes as it goes on, the more I realize that it involves an unsurprisingly unsexy amount of just normal 'work' stuff.

"Work stuff?" you may ask, "define work stuff..?"

Well, first of all, the whale sharks, the octopus, the smiling faces, the epic boat rides, the unexpected new friendships, the crazy cool challenges and the unforgettable sunsets are indeed all real. They really are. I hope that my previous statements didn't give you the impression that none of that exists. It's just that more often than not, we may also have to choose to forgo a magical sunset for actual work stuff.

If we don't spend hours going through our underwater footage and take the time to edit them, post them and write captivating captions, not a whole lot of people will know we even exist and our mailbox will soon be empty.

If we don't take time to sit down and answer our emails once or twice daily, very few of those inquiries will actually convert into new students. And believe me: even in the best of times it takes an ungodly amount of answered emails to result in a booking.

If we don't properly enter our bookings and make hotel reservations, plan our staff, create a course schedule and review our materials, these customers aren't going to be exactly happy with their experience, much less stay and continue diving with us.

If we don't practice our lesson plans, study up on the latest SCUBA diving trends and entertain our clients with knowledge and passion, those end-of-day sunset drinks won't mean very much to them.

 It's understandable that most popular SCUBA instructors / social media influencers don't really highlight the boring stuff. You'd certainly be forgiven for thinking that the crazy adventures in the blue are all they really do. Let's hope that now you've come to understand that hard, boring and tedious tasks are just as much a part of the job as the cool stuff.

Of course, you may very well be getting into this game to find a part time gig, or as a retirement plan, or simply because you have plenty of other sources of revenue and want this to be more of a hobby. That is of course possible and respectable. Just remember that in the SCUBA industry, input very much equals output.

4.3. The Right Kind of Hard Work

There is nothing wrong with hard work, by the way. It's the repetitive, tedious, hard work for a project you don't fully believe in that's insufferable to most people. In general, most of us don't mind putting in the hard work when the work directly aligns with our passion.

The greatest thing to do in life is to find something you're actually passionate about and then go all in!

That being said, nothing is 100% fun. Nothing is 100% easy or enjoyable. However, the more you lean into what makes your heart beat faster, the easier it will be to motivate yourself for the subtasks you may not like.

As a rule of thumb, I always try to analyze whether something is around 70-80% 'fun'. If the answer is yes, you're probably in line with your passion. Jobs that are 100% fun simply don't exist. I doubt many actors are deeply excited to sit through casting calls, or study their lines over and over. I doubt that painters very much enjoy negotiating with galleries about the commissions they will take for displaying their art. If something is presented as too much fun or too easy, chances are someone is trying to sell you snake oil.

The idea that work shouldn't feel like work is a dangerous one. So rather than wondering whether a task feels like 'work' or not, it's worth just considering whether it contributes to something you are really excited about. If the answer is yes, I think you can safely assume you're on the right track.

Keep in mind that things also won't always work out the way you intended, even if what you're doing aligns with your heart's desire. As mentioned earlier, we often witness the success stories without truly seeing the hard work behind them. Similarly, for every visible and advertised success story, there are likely many trial and errors that came before it that simply aren't as sexy to talk about.

 Your first SCUBA job may not be the job of your dreams. Your first thousand photos as an underwater photographer are likely to be terrible and your initial teaching- and guiding style may not be as universally admired as you would hope. Once again, persistence is key. And don't be afraid to fail terribly along the way.

A moment of silence and reflection
before a technical dive

Photo by Ashley Kirkham / College of Diving

Ancient rock formations in
a Mexican Cenote

Photo by Carolina Wells

Close up of a Blue Shark in the Azores, Portugal

Photo by Nick Derutter

Caught in the action during a technical diving course in Utila

Photo by Gil Sassi / College of Diving

GET
STARTED

5. Writing a Good SCUBA Resume

It takes on average seven subsequent positive impressions to correct a first negative impression, and your first contact with a potential employer may very well be your resume. I'm very passionate about this topic and actually spend a lot of time with my instructor candidates on supporting them to create an above-average CV.

5.1. Content

As a popular employer, we see hundreds of CV's every year, and as far as content goes, let me give you some do's and don'ts that should help you get started.

DO

- Name, date of birth, nationality.
- Picture (although unusual in other industries, it's very common in SCUBA diving)
- Training agency and pro member number (that allows us to do a little check on you)
- Professional diving certifications. Start with the highest first, sided by the year you achieved it. Don't forget your specialty instructor certifications, probably leading with the most unique ones on top to show employers what sets you apart.
- Other extra curricular skills you may have. Perhaps you're a TEFL teacher (Teaching English as a Foreign Language), perhaps you're a website designer, an equipment technician or a boat mechanic. Even if we're not looking for a dive instructor who happens to also be a yoga teacher, it does tell us something about previous teaching experience, your passions and what kind of person we have in front of us.
- Languages: If you speak or are able to teach in multiple languages, be sure to highlight this. It's huge! Be honest and indicate which one is your native language, which ones are conversational and which are rather basic.
- Any relevant work experience. Perhaps you've recently had a sales position or worked as a team leader. All of this gives us information about the position we could be hiring you for.

- What are you looking for? Are you ready to commit for a year or two, or are you rather looking for a seasonal position? Do you mind teaching entry level courses or does your level of experience mean that you're ready for a more high profile position? What are your ambitions in diving and what would you like to get out of a job?

DON'T

- While it's great to have some pictures of you in your dive outfit, if that's the only one and your face is covered by a mask, it makes it hard to see who we're dealing with.
- Spelling mistakes (this should go without saying but it's incredibly common)
- Multiple pages. Two pages should be the absolute maximum and even that's a stretch, unless your list of relevant credentials really takes up this much space.
- If you are sending your resume out to multiple potential employers, hide them in BCC or even better: send each one an individual and personalized email. We like to feel special. Let us know why you want to work for us specifically. Sending a resume with all of our competitors in CC just suggests laziness on your part.

5.2. Layout

Layout is super important but stick to something basic and don't get carried away. Over the years I've seen some impressive CV's, though you would be surprised at how many of them are drafted up in five minutes on Wordpad with zero thought to how they look.

We're (probably) not looking for a graphic designer but a proper layout, consistent font use, appropriate capitalization and reasonably sized pictures go a long way in letting us know how you work in general. If your potential employer is looking for someone motivated, organized and professional, they will probably (maybe subconsciously) make a pre-selection purely based on the thought you've put into making your resume.

If you're sending in a digital resume, convert it to PDF first, rather than sending a word document. Word documents don't cross over well between Mac and PC, can be difficult to open on phones and often reformat themselves. PDF is definitely the way to go.

5.3. Cover letter

While a CV does a great job at clearly summarizing who you are in terms of your credentials and experience, the truth is that two very different people could obtain very similar credentials.

A CV only goes so far in letting a potential employer know who you are and what you are looking for. Besides fleshing out who you are as a person, a cover letter is also a great instrument for detailing why you want to work for a specific company.

Most cover letters are best kept to one page or shorter, unless the job position requires you to write something longer. Keep it to the point and engaging, while ensuring that it is not a generic letter. This is your chance to be authentic.

5.4. Classic mistakes

As I mentioned, I read hundreds of resumes every year. It's truly remarkable how almost every single CV always has one of the same five or six mistakes. Let's go over them, so you can easily avoid making those same mistakes.

Font choice can go a long way. You have some leeway in that choice but the most common choices are Times New Roman or some variation thereof or Arial or a variation. I receive a surprising amount of resumes in Comic Sans. I thought it was common sense that this is the world's most hated font. I guess I was wrong.
Spelling mistakes are also very common but a big no no. Afterall, a CV is a one-page document and it should be relatively straightforward to spell check it before sending it off.

Another frequent mistake is that when people include their professional ratings, they tend to paraphrase on the nomenclature of those ratings. For instance: if you are a "Peak Performance Buoyancy Instructor", call it that. Don't write "Peak Buoyancy". It's really a small effort to look up the correct terminology.

One of the most mind blowing common mistakes is the omittance of contact information. I receive several resumes each year with no phone number whatsoever. While it is understandable that you may have just arrived in a foreign land, looking for employment, it's also understandable that I won't call you if you can't give me a phone number. Email address is an option but it's a very slow way of communicating and you could really lose out on a great opportunity if you're not readily available.

As mentioned above, most industries these days don't ask (or are not allowed to ask) for a photo. That's perfectly understandable but in the SCUBA industry it is commonplace to insert a photo of yourself. Make sure that photo is clear. A surprising majority of the CV's I read, come with a single photo in which the applicant is in full SCUBA gear, mask and all, which makes it very hard to see who's applying.

When listing your education and work history, it's okay to be brief. Most industries will expect your resume to be quite complete in the sense of previous employment or formal education but in the SCUBA industry it may not matter as much. It's certainly okay to mention it but if it's not relevant, don't elaborate too much. It distracts from your SCUBA credentials and other relevant skills and can make the CV overly long.

SCUBA Resume Information Checklist

Name
Nationality
Date of Birth
E-mail
Phone

Teaching status: YES/NO	INSURANCE: YES/NO

Certification level_____ since_____ Course taken at_____

Cert count _____ students certified

Specialty Instructor Ratings

Languages

About me

Relevant Work Experience

Position:_____ at _____ from_____ to _____
Position:_____ at _____ from_____ to _____

NICK
DERUTTER
PADI Course Director #282240

About Me

I'm a PADI Platinum Course Director available for immediate employment in a busy 5 Star Career Development Center. I'm able to commit to a one-year contract or longer, depending on the job description. My goals are to be part of a dynamic team that can offer a broad range of recreational and professional training, as well as technical and adaptive SCUBA diving. Due to my background as a hyperbaric chamber operator and hundreds of hours of operator and supervisor time, I have a strong interest towards hyperbaric medicine and diver safety.

 Belgium

 May 18, 1984

 +123-456-7890

 nick@divesaga.com

123 Anywhere St., Any City

QUALIFICATIONS

- PADI Platinum Course Director (3000+certs) 2014
- PADI Master SCUBA Diver Trainer 2011
- Emergency First Response Trainer 2010
- Tec Deep Instructor Trainer 2016
- Tec Trimix Instructor Trainer 2019
- Diveheart Adaptive Instructor Trainer 2016
- ANDI Hyperbaric Chamber Operator Trainer 2016

SPECIALTY INSTRUCTOR RATINGS

- Enriched Air Diver
- Fullface Mask Diver
- Sidemount Diver
- Tec Sidemount Diver
- Dry Suit
- Emergency Oxygen Provider
- Wreck Diver
- Deep Diver
- Digital Underwater Photography
- Underwater Videography
- Underwater Navigator
- Night Diver
- Search & Recovery
- Fish ID
- Self Reliant Diver
- Distinctive Field Neurological Exam
- TecRec Gas Blender Nitrox & Trimix

LANGUAGE

- English
- Dutch
- French
- Spanish
- German (basic)

REFERENCES

John Doe
Dive Shop Manager

+123 456-789
info@johndoediveshop.com

5.5. Online Interviews

It's not unusual that, after you send in your resume, an employer will invite you to an online call to get a better feel for who you are and to discuss what you both expect from each other.

It's obviously a good idea to be on time for this (check your time zones) and to find a place with a decent internet connection if you're globe trotting. I've been involved in dozens of calls where the connection was just too bad and even though I did my best to not let this influence my opinion on the candidate, it subconsciously did, I'm sure.

Dress appropriately, put on a shirt, look rested, put away that cigarette and go find a quiet location for the call. Again, this should all go without saying.

Prepare yourself and write down what your expectations are. While you probably really want to get that first job, people will respect you for knowing what you want, if it's reasonable. An interview is a waste of time for both parties if it's not clear what you expect from one another.

Use the following worksheet as a tool to prepare yourself for the interview. You won't necessarily be expected to answer these questions but it's always a good idea to have information like this ready to go, in case it comes up.

Interview Preparation Worksheet

Use this worksheet to write down the answers to some commonly asked questions.

How and why did my previous job position come to an end?

What is the maximum time commitment I'm willing to give to this job?

What do I expect from my job description?

What are my short term ambitions?

What are my long term goals?

What are my strengths?

What are my weaknesses? (no cheating, REAL weaknesses only!)

How is hiring me going to be a positive addition to the dive center?

Give an example of a work related moment you are proud of

Give an example of situation where you applied great problem solving

You messed up and a customer is unhappy with your performance. What do you do?

What are my expectations in regards to payment?

5.6. Manage your social media

By now it's probably no secret that after reading a resume and cover letter, some employers may snoop through the Facebook or Instagram profiles of potential employees. They'll do this to get a closer look at the person they're dealing with and perhaps see how they fill their time outside of SCUBA diving. If some of your adventures aren't suitable for publication, you might want to not make them public.

Secondly, you may want to think about making a second Facebook profile for your SCUBA diving activities. This shares a double purpose: firstly it makes it a little bit more manageable to choose how you 'display' yourself to potential future employers but secondly, this could also be the page that you allow students to befriend you on.

When I started off as a SCUBA instructor, I put very little thought into this and, naturally, students started sending me friend requests on Facebook, which I gladly accepted. Now, years later, I find myself with a massive database of past and future divers on my personal Facebook page, which forces me to censor myself and be very selective about what I post because "potential customers" are watching.

Yes, it's double the work but you'll be able to separate work and private much better and, perhaps more importantly, you'll be much more able to target your divers with dive-related posts that will make them want to come back and train with you. For potential employers it's also a great way to get a very specific look into your SCUBA dealings.

5.7. The internet as a personal marketing tool

If the previous section has put you off of the idea of adding your dive students to your friends list, think again. If used correctly (a separate profile, as mentioned above) Facebook can actually be a very powerful tool for diver retention.

Let the people in your network know that you are now a SCUBA instructor and show them what a fun time they can have with you. On your dedicated SCUBA page, you can create 'Events' and invite former students to join your next scheduled classes. Offer incentives for divers to return to you and tag your current students in photos.

Visual marketing used to be a complex endeavor and getting good, high quality images was the work of a professional photographer. These days, almost all of us have at least 15 megapixels on the flipside of our phone and high definition video on our tic tac-container-sized Gopro camera. There is no excuse not to show the world the kinds of fun you are having with your students.

The opposite is also true. Make sure your students know to tag you (your SCUBA profile) in their SCUBA adventure photos and do some of the marketing for you. As a start, Facebook and Instagram are great platforms to start building an audience and at the same time offering potential employers an insight into your teaching work.

When my personal Instagram account surpassed 1000 followers, I decided to turn it into a business account and post SCUBA related content only. In just a matter of a few years, it grew into its own brand with over 30.000 followers and lots of training inquiries. In many ways, the simple act of taking care of social media started generating its own opportunities in the industry.

Don't forget to follow us @divesaga!

Did You Know?

Even though the oceans are all interconnected, invasive species are a real issue in certain areas. The venomous lionfish, for instance, is a ruthless predator that is decimating other fish species in the Caribbean. Luckily they are a tasty food to humans!

6. How to Land Your Dream Job

We discussed earlier that choosing a training center that fits your personal style is important for a good start to your professional career, it's also immensely important to apply only at those dive centers where you truly see yourself working and growing. It's very easy to become just another work horse looking for just another job to pass the time and make some money. However, for the right place with the right vibe, you could be a genuine gem that could drive the company forward by being a key player on the team.

You should probably ask yourself why you're in the SCUBA diving industry.

- Do you want to live a calm and quiet life while teaching a few students per week and be happy with a fee that helps you get by just fine?

- Are you perhaps looking to gain a lot of experience quickly by working hard every day, double, triple teaching and experiencing the outer limits of your capabilities?

- Is it time to increase your own skills and are you looking to move up the ranks and take on a managerial position?

Whatever the answer to these questions, some dive centers will fit the bill better than others and in the long run no one benefits from a mismatch.

 A friend of mine worked in a resort in Mexico for one year, conducting over 2000 Discover Scuba Diving experiences with first time divers. He didn't do this because he took the first job he could get (honestly, he wouldn't have lasted a year). Instead he did it to push his patience to the limit to become the best instructor he could possibly be, while saving up 50.000 USD that year to further improve his own skills and open up some new traveling opportunities.

Whatever it is you're looking for, make sure you know what you want and direct all your energy towards it.

It may be interesting to have a look at the following map. This is an interactive job placement map. I use it to keep track of some of the people that I have trained and where they went on to find their first SCUBA job. One might expect that, since they all trained at the same place, they might all end up following similar career tracks. Instead, you'll see that they ended up spread out across the globe pretty evenly.

No two career paths are identical and it's only by sticking to what really excites you and doing what you really want to do, that you'll be good and successful.

JOB PLACEMENT MAP

6.1. Applying Locally

Applying for a job from abroad is an immensely time consuming process but it's not impossible and we'll talk more about that in the next chapter.

For now, let's focus on landing a job in your immediate area. Whether this is your home base or a foreign location you happen to be staying at the moment, if this is where you want to work, then being on the spot is an excellent advantage!

Diving is a very personal and social activity and when we hire new instructors, we like to know who we have in front of us. In our dive school, we only hire the best but we also have an "ideal cast" of instructors that we like to see working for us at any given moment. We always want to have a tech-savvy nerd on board, as well as a happy go-lucky bon vivant. We enjoy having local people on the team who can give our guests a sense of 'island culture' that others can't, as well as some more mature instructors who appeal to a very specific crowd. Call it 'type casting', if you will. (Our manager is also adamant on having a 'James Bond-like figure' on the team and apparently I fit the bill. I won't complain!)

It's not unusual for a well-ran dive school to strive to have an eclectic staff and by being on the spot and walking in, talking to the staff and the management, you'll give them the opportunity to start thinking about how you might fit in. Timing is of course everything. Make sure that when you go and offer your services you get to speak to whoever is in charge of the hiring of staff. This is crucial and just leaving a resume behind at the front desk is probably a waste of time and resources.

Another advantage of being on the spot, handing out a resume with a local phone number and checking in frequently, is that if there's a sudden influx of business beyond what the staff can handle, they may call upon you for some freelance work. On many occasions have we hired people because they were available, flexible and happy to take any small job and make it work. As usual, above everything, make sure your performance is top notch!

6.2. Applying From Abroad

Part of taking the advice I gave previously and really thinking about and deciding what sort of a career you would like, might mean that your local area simply doesn't offer the type of dive school you want to work for. That's okay, you'll simply have to expand your action perimeter and apply for positions abroad.

Finding job offers online is the easy part. Websites such as www.divezone.net/jobs or www.diversjobs.com as well as member forums on the website of your selected training agency are great starting points for your job search. Through our SAGA Instructor Network, we also offer dedicated job placement after training. This means that whenever someone graduates and we think they might fit in well with a place we know, we provide the initial introduction. When some of our former graduates work at a place that is looking to hire, they usually let us know and we make it known within the network. It's a very powerful way of getting a foot in the door!

Once you've made a shortlist of some of the recent job offers that caught your attention and fit your personal ambitions, it's time to do some quick research. Visit the website of each individual dive shop and try to get a good understanding of how they operate and double check that this is a place you could see yourself working for. Check their location and if airline tickets are not part of the compensation package that's offered, do a quick online check to see whether airfare to that destination fits within your personal budget.

Now it's time to start writing a personalized application letter to each one of them. Include a paragraph about what you admire about their operation and why you think you'd be the best person for the job. Be genuine and honest, make sure to attach that killer resume you made after reading chapter 4 and let them know when you would be available for an online interview, following the rules of chapter 4.4.

Check your mailbox often and reply promptly!

6.3. Working for a big training center

There are essentially two approaches to deciding what type of dive operation you should choose for employment. Neither one of them is wrong, but knowing yourself is key and depending on your own character, you may prefer either or.

The first approach would be to look for those dive centers that are well established, have a solid team and hierarchy in place and advertise themselves as such.

The benefit of working for an operation like this is that you'll be surrounded by structure and experience, and for some of us, this may forever shape the way we conduct ourselves as a diving professional. You'll have peers from which to get guidance during your first months on the job, and the methods that are used by all are probably standardized and proven - beyond whatever the training agency dictates. This means you'll be picking up a lot of great habits and you'll have the opportunity to grow slowly into a well-rounded professional.

Another benefit of working for a training center like this, is that you'll most likely have all kinds of additional training available to you and you'll be able to further your own education and learn on the job.

The drawback, however, is that oftentimes the competition to work at these well-oiled machines may be pretty substantial. Unless you have some exceptional skills and a built-up resume, it may not be all that easy to get hired right away.

6.4. Working for a small dive operation

The second approach to starting to build your own career is to find a relatively small dive operation and immediately assume a relatively large role. This is easier in smaller operations because they may not have a rigid command structure like the bigger ones.

If you're an individual who is relatively self directed, ambitious and you have been able to enjoy a proper professional training, it may be a great challenge to help build up a smaller dive center into something big. You'll be much more able to make your mark and run things the way you like to (with respect to the owners of the operation) and you may soon be able to assemble a team that works closely with you and learns from you.

The drawback here is that you need to be very aware of your own abilities. Almost all new SCUBA instructors will make mistakes and having no solid entourage of experienced professionals around you, may mean that you start developing 'bad habits' without realizing it. Make sure the training you have received is solid and adhere to it closely. If you do this, building a smaller dive operation from the ground up by working closely with owners or managers may be an amazing experience that will allow you to push the limits of your own abilities and help you make your mark on the industry.

Did You Know?

SCUBA divers roll off the boat backwards because if they would roll forward, they would still be in the boat.

7. Common Mistakes on the Job

7.1. The laws of physics still apply

One of my favorite quotes that a PADI Instructor Examiner once said to newly certified SCUBA instructors was "Contrary to what most of you may suddenly think, unfortunately the laws of physics still apply to you now that you are a dive instructor. Stay safe!"

You'll be doing multiple dives per day, multiple days per week and that's an amazing way to make a living. Unfortunately, this doesn't exempt you from the physical challenges every diver faces when entering the water and creating a potential for drowning or breathing compressed air and creating a potential for barotrauma.

What most divers fail to understand about decompression sickness is that there is actually no such thing as an "undeserved hit" of DCS. If you have been SCUBA diving, you can get DCS, even when you did everything right. That's because even the most conservative prediction model still works "probabilities", meaning you probably won't get DCS after executing a certain profile but "probably" doesn't mean "definitely" and it's a very important distinction to make.

A very important thing you can do to reduce your risk of decompression sickness is of course make every dive as conservative as possible. You do this not just by using the more conservative settings on your computer but also by limiting your dive depths to only what's "necessary" for the job, by staying very hydrated throughout the day and by exercising regularly (although not immediately before and after your dives).

Multiple ascents and descents in a dive and multiple dives in a row will still increase your risk of decompression sickness and there's simply nothing a certification card can do to change that. Take care of yourself and stay aware of your profiles, the state of your equipment and signals you're getting from your own body. Your body is the most highly advanced piece of equipment you'll ever own and you'll only ever get one.

Perhaps now is a good time to learn about diving accidents. What follows are some interesting recreational SCUBA diving incident statistics to look at, which can lend us some perspective into what divers die from, how they die, what the contributing factors are and how we, as diving professionals can help prevent them.

90%	DIED WITH THEIR WEIGHT BELT ON
86%	WERE ALONE WHEN THEY DIED (SOLO DIVING OR SEPARATED)
50%	DID NOT INFLATE THEIR BCD
25%	FIRST GOT INTO DIFFICULTY ON THE SURFACE
50%	DIED ON THE SURFACE
10%	WERE UNDER TRAINING WHEN THEY DIED
10%	HAD BEEN ADVISED THEY WERE MEDICALLY UNFIT TO DIVE
5%	WERE CAVE DIVING
1%	OF DIVERS ATTEMPTING A RESCUE DIED AS A RESULT

Source: Diving fatality data published in Diving Medicine for SCUBA Divers (2015)

To interpret the next two graphs, it's important to make a distinction between the "trigger" of the accident and the "cause of death". The "trigger" is the incident that sets off the chain of events that causes the accident and the "cause of death" ultimately being the medical condition that the injured diver died from.

I decided to include these in this book because as a diving professional, you have an inherent responsibility over yourself and the divers you supervise. One of the critical errors you can make in your career, going forward, is not paying sufficient attention to the most common causes of diving incidents and failing to modify your professional activities to mitigate these risks.

MOST COMMON TRIGGERS FOR DIVER FATALITY

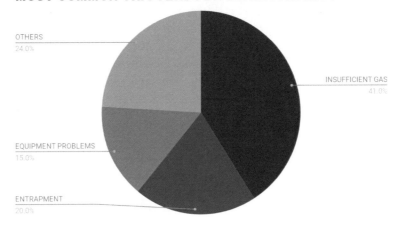

OTHERS
24.0%

INSUFFICIENT GAS
41.0%

EQUIPMENT PROBLEMS
15.0%

ENTRAPMENT
20.0%

Source: DAN study (2008) with compiled data from 947 recreational open-circuit SCUBA diving deaths between 1992 and 2003

MOST COMMON CAUSE OF DIVER DEATH

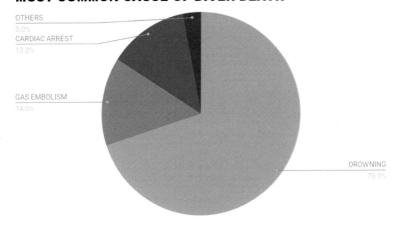

OTHERS
3.0%
CARDIAC ARREST
13.0%

GAS EMBOLISM
14.0%

DROWNING
70.0%

Source: DAN study (2008) with compiled data from 947 recreational open-circuit SCUBA diving deaths between 1992 and 2003

7.2. Knowing your limits

The environment you'll be teaching in won't necessarily be the same environment you were trained in and that's okay. Divers obtain local orientations from more experienced divers all the time. In fact, it's the proper way to do things. Don't be afraid to cancel a dive for any reason whatsoever and follow your instincts. Dive students may think you owe them a certification card but what you really owe them is your time and a safe and controlled learning environment.

 Don't let anyone ever force you into making poor decisions, not even your own ambitions. While it's a tough call to tell a new employer on your first job that you don't feel comfortable teaching that group of six people all at once, it's the only right thing to do. Nobody wins from you taking on too much too soon.

Good employers should realize that new instructors need time to grow and so should you. Start by teaching one or –at most- two students (ideally by team teaching with an experienced instructor) and don't allow yourself to dive or teach in conditions you aren't experienced with.

Worried about losing that first job? It's better to lose this one job, than to kill someone and lose every job opportunity ever.

The best way to learn your limits is by taking on an internship with the dive school that trained you to become a SCUBA instructor. Most dive schools will run an internship program where you'll have the ability to get hands-on experience in running a variety of smaller and bigger courses under the guidance of an experienced staff member. This will give you a clear indication of what you are and aren't ready for. Yet!

7.3. Don't skip the prep

Just like teachers in elementary school or college professors, you'll need to do your homework and make a lesson plan. You should never expect to rock up at work and just push the 'teach-button'. Well run courses are the result of thorough preparation. You may remember something about preparation being a key characteristic for an instructor in chapter 1.

Even though you may be an instructor now, if you're teaching a course tomorrow, whether it's Open Water Diver or a Stress and Rescue course, you're going to want to do all the exact same homework your students are doing. You'll want to watch the same videos, answer the same study questions and try the same exams. This will give you a realistic insight into what information they will be getting from the study materials and where you will probably have to elaborate. Knowing the student materials inside out is simply a matter of being a good teacher.

Furthermore, it never hurts to be one or multiple steps ahead of your students. Meaning you should always know more than what is laid out in the curriculum you are teaching. This will allow you to answer unexpected questions or shed light on themes that aren't necessarily handled in the materials but may peak your student's interests.

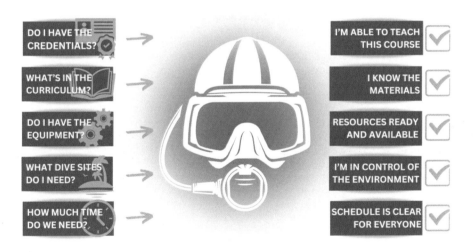

DO I HAVE THE CREDENTIALS? → I'M ABLE TO TEACH THIS COURSE ✓

WHAT'S IN THE CURRICULUM? → I KNOW THE MATERIALS ✓

DO I HAVE THE EQUIPMENT? → RESOURCES READY AND AVAILABLE ✓

WHAT DIVE SITES DO I NEED? → I'M IN CONTROL OF THE ENVIRONMENT ✓

HOW MUCH TIME DO WE NEED? → SCHEDULE IS CLEAR FOR EVERYONE ✓

7.4. Use your materials

Another big mistake that can be easily prevented is giving in to the urge to teach without the proper materials on you while you teach. Most training agencies provide instructors with a set of plastic underwater slates or laminated cue cards that can be used during the training dives to double check the requirements for each training session as you are teaching.

There is nothing weird about carrying these materials on your person while conducting your classes. On the contrary, in fact: this will always give you a point of reference on how to conduct the curriculum and will suggest to your students that you are delivering the complete course without skipping steps.

Teaching without the proper instructional materials will lead to omitted content and will set you on a path of forming the wrong habits. This will eventually push you in a situation where it will become hard to defend your actions in case of a potential incident. One of the single most common complaints any given training agency receives after course completion is that steps were skipped, skills were omitted and training was actually incomplete. Don't short change your students.

Did You Know?

Octopus arms have a mind of their own. Two-thirds of an octopus' neurons reside in its arms, not its head. As a result, the arms can problem solve how to open a shellfish while the rest of the octopus can perform other complex tasks!

8. When Things Go Wrong

8.1. Your Reputation

Maintaining a positive reputation throughout the industry is your first line of defense for when things go wrong. This line of defense should be established well before something ever does go wrong and can hopefully serve as a testament to your character and positive demeanor towards the sport and its participants.

So how do I establish 'a positive reputation'?

Curating a positive image about yourself and your SCUBA dealings is more than just smoke and mirrors. We are not talking about making people believe you are professional, we are talking about actually BEING professional.

Make sure your course offerings are priced straightforward and honest. Ensure the course contents are complete and diligent. Be available and friendly to potential customers. Treat your students and fellow divers with courtesy and respect, regardless of their background. Stay in reasonable physical and mental shape. And above all: If you get to a point where you can't work as a diver any longer (be it temporary or definitive): don't!

As SCUBA instructors we are usually on the front line of training. Yes, training agencies write the curriculum and dive centers may be the business and logistics hub but we, the individual diving educators, are the ones who are right there in the classrooms, in the pools and in the open water. When things go wrong, they usually go wrong in the field and we are often the only ones who are truly right there. It is then no surprise that, even though victims of SCUBA related incidents often sue multiple entities, the dive instructor is the most vulnerable entity in this situation.

Communicating clearly and teaching safe and comprehensive, complete courses is key to remaining above reproach. Professionalism is about what you do. Every day. While having a professional reputation isn't a 100% effective firewall against accidents or lawsuits, it goes a long way in telling a story about your character and in the prevention of accidents in the first place.

8.2. In the Event of and Accident

Unfortunately, accidents are unavoidable. You can absolutely stack the deck in your favor with some simple steps:

- Evaluate whether you are ready to teach that specific course in that specific situation.
- Evaluate your student's readiness to start and progress in the course.
- Evaluate the environmental conditions every time you teach.
- Ensure you have enough time available for each course.
- Ensure all equipment is in proper working order.
- Look and listen for signs of anxiety with your students.
- Never operate close to any limits (depths, student ratios, ascent rates, bottom times, etc)
- When you're not sure about something: cancel the dive.

Again: accidents are unavoidable but we can try to minimize them. Unfortunately, every time people are engaging in water activities there is a potential for drowning. Every time people are breathing compressed gas under water there is a potential for gas expansion injuries.

If you do find yourself involved in a SCUBA diving accident, there are some things you can do to mitigate the situation.

- Firstly and most importantly, be ready and equipped to offer every reasonable amount of first aid. Having (and regularly checking) oxygen kits, first aid kits and other relevant rescue equipment is key.
- Do not put yourself in harm's way when trying to defuse a dangerous situation. Making reasonable rescue efforts is crucial and part of your duty of care but differentiate between a reasonable effort and a foolish or dangerous endeavor that can make the situation worse. Adding yourself to the list of victims only makes the situation worse and spreads the available resources more thin.

- Do not make statements about blame, including about yourself. Even if you think a situation may be your fault, or you feel emotionally compelled to volunteer responsibility, it is not advisable. It is neither helpful, nor smart and there will definitely be future investigations that can eventually indicate who is responsible.
- Contact your lawyer. As a precautionary step, it's wise to figure out who you would call in the event of a SCUBA diving accident so you know who to contact if it does happen. Follow their advice on what to do or not do and say or not say.
- Contact your insurance company. We have discussed the virtues of professional liability and diving accident insurance. This is where you may need to use them. Involve them early on.
- Remain involved. Once involved in an accident, do not 'disappear'. While it's not advisable to share your observations or opinions with anyone at all, it may be required to share your observed facts with law enforcement.
- Make a mental note of potential witnesses and how to contact them and locate and secure training paperwork that may be needed.

Remember: just because you are involved in a SCUBA diving related accident, does not mean you are in trouble. Do whatever you reasonably can to maintain a professional and calm demeanor throughout.

If your students or fellow divers do report injury or discomfort during or after a dive, take it seriously. Direct them to the appropriate medical professionals. You are not a physician but they may be looking for your endorsement to go see one. Being encouraged to go talk to a doctor when it's not needed has far less severe consequences than being dissuaded from seeing one when it is needed!

 Do not obsess over the 'what-ifs' of diving accidents but keep the potential for accidents on your mind in your daily dealings. This will go a long way in catching them well before they happen.

8.3. Sexual Harassment

We need to talk about sexual harassment and inappropriate behavior on the work floor in SCUBA diving. I am sad to say that the diving industry is unfortunately not free of this type of behavior.

Unfortunately it's not hard to imagine that in an environment where people's daily attire is often just whatever swimwear they use, some people may lose perspective on what appropriate boundaries are. And just to be clear: I don't mean to make 'losing perspective' sound like it's not their fault, because it is!

Whether we are talking from instructor to student or vice versa is irrelevant, but since you're reading this book as an aspiring SCUBA instructor, let's assume the scenario where that's what you are. As an instructor you are in a position where you have a duty of care, physically and emotionally. At the same time you are also in a position where you need to get close to your students for safety and control. SCUBA diving can be a close contact sport and there is nothing wrong with that, if certain rules are respected.

 This should probably go without saying but you should treat your students with equality and respect, regardless of their gender, age, race or background. They are here with you because they have decided to step out of their comfort zone and learn something new. Something that may be frightening to many people. They are with you because they have decided that you as a person, the institution you work for or the training agency you represent has a reputation that they trust. It's your job to not damage that trust.

Let's take the example of breathing without a mask underwater for the very first time. Students often feel blinded and isolated during this skill and I often offer to place my hand on their shoulder during the process so they have a point of reference during this maneuver. The crucial element here is that I OFFER to place a hand on their shoulder. Some may want that reassurance, some may prefer to be left to themselves to work through that skill. Imagine a scenario where you are a female student, removing a mask and breathing without it underwater for the very first time and suddenly, out of nowhere, a hand slides on top of your shoulder or the side of your arm. The instructor's intention may be perfectly pure (or not) but nobody wants to have to struggle through no-mask breathing while trying to simultaneously figure out whether they are in an awkward situation or not. Very clearly offering physical support is crucial, including the option to decline it (unless safety critically requires it).

Similarly, it is crucial to properly brief the steps involved in all SCUBA skills. A student who clearly understands what needs to be accomplished, will better understand why certain physical actions may be required. Do what's needed to make your students feel at ease. If you're teaching a class where close physical contact is unavoidable (for instance CPR training where you're expected to perform an abdominal thrust on someone of the opposite gender) it is proper form to explain the mechanics of the skill, ask the student if they are comfortable with this type of contact, or find a staff member of the same gender they may be more comfortable with. A little bit of smart scheduling and a lot of clear communication can avoid a lot of uncomfortable situations. Remember: if you are consistently professional in all your offerings, your students probably won't assume your intentions are bad.

You may also find yourself in a situation where the student initiates inappropriate rhetoric or behavior in the direction of the instructor. Unfortunately some students interpret the physicality of the training as an invitation to overstep certain boundaries. Once again these boundaries can be made clear by clear communication and professionalism but that doesn't mean that unacceptable behavior from your students is due to a lack of professionalism on your part.

As an instructor you are never expected to stay in a situation in which you are not respected. As adults we can all differentiate between a panicked student grabbing you because they are sincerely in need of support and students who are abusing the training context to establish unnecessary physical contact. Signal this. They pay you for proper instruction and safety but nothing else. communicate potential problems early to your colleagues and, if you're able, to the students themselves.

Keeping a healthy working, teaching and learning environment for everyone involved is a collaborative effort. Support your colleagues in their professionalism, don't make comments about people's bodies, don't use patronizing or condescending language and maintain a culture of open communication.

While inappropriate behavior from male to female is much, much more common, the opposite is not non-existent. I've been in several situations where female students slapped male instructors on the butt, or made lewd comments about their appearance. Say something. A professional, harassment-free environment can only exist if it exists across the board.

When given no path to amicable resolve, do not hesitate to pursue other avenues to make it stop. Being harassed does not mean you did something wrong, failed to signal boundaries or were lacking professionalism.

Shooting our YouTube episode
'Finding Snooty' in Jupiter, FL

Photo by Gil Sassi

In the shallow jungle waters of cenote 'Ponderosa' in Mexico

Photo by Tom St Georges

Checking the dry glove seal before
Ice Diver Course final training dive
in Lake Superior, Michigan

Photo by Rich Synowiec

The cloud below is Hydrogen Sulfide gas, formed by decomposing leafs in Cenote Angelita, Mexico

Photo by Carolina Wells

GET BETTER

9. Safeguard Your Future – Visa, Insurance and Retirement

That's a boring title for a chapter if there ever was one! However, remember that you are reading this book because you want to do things right. Teaching SCUBA, just like any other job, will always have more longevity if your t's are crossed and your i's are dotted.

9.1. Work visa

If you're looking to work in your local area then this chapter is non-applicable, but for those who are in search of a more international lifestyle, some thought will have to go into obtaining legal working permits.

Let's address the elephant in the room here. A lot of tropical diving takes place in locations where local authorities often can't or aren't too concerned with enforcing immigration policies. They recognize that the diving industry is a big contributor to local tourism income and turn a blind eye to it. This book is in no way encouraging you to work abroad in this way, nor am I taking a stance on the legal and moral implications of this.

There are many options to work in a diving paradise legally. Because there are around 190 countries and that would make 190 x 190 possible combinations of "nationality x" working in "country x", it is impossible for me to give you all 36.100 working visa application rules. These rules also tend to change frequently so you will have to do some of your own research online or contact consulates or embassies.

For citizens of the European Union, it shouldn't be overly hard to work in other member states of the Union, so there's that. British citizens may find it relatively easy to obtain a permit for overseas territories, such as the British Virgin Islands for instance. The same usually applies for citizens from other countries with overseas departments, such as The Netherlands or France.

Some countries have working-holiday visa programs that will grant you a one or two year working permit. Countries like

Canada, Australia, New-Zealand, South Africa and others are worth looking into.

In many countries it's also possible to simply obtain a working permit through local sponsorship, for instance. My best advice is to consult with other people working in the local area and see how they do it. It never hurts to consult a local law expert and look into what options are available for you.

Many people live and work in paradise and so can you. You just need to get through the red tape.

9.2. Medical insurance

The best couple-hundred-bucks per year you'll spend when working as a dive instructor, will be those on a medical insurance plan. It's a small investment and, really, you would hope to never need to cash in on that investment but it's a nice feeling, knowing that someone's got your back.

When divers get hurt, the medical cost can be significant. Many injuries such as decompression sickness and certain lung overexpansion injuries can require treatment in a hyperbaric chamber. Running a hyperbaric chamber alongside our dive center and being an operator myself, I can tell you: treatments don't come cheap. A standard 'NAVY table 6' treatment with around five hours of recompression and two to three hours of medical preparation and follow up, make the operating costs of these facilities quite high and a single treatment can cost several thousands of dollars. When you imagine that it's not unusual for patients to require multiple treatments (I've known of cases requiring up to fourteen treatments) the costs involved with hyperbaric treatment can be astronomical and carrying insurance that will cover these costs will pay off immediately, even after one hit.

Add to this that not every dive environment has immediate access to a hyperbaric facility and that treatment should be administered "as soon as possible" (more than 24 hours is too late) and you will understand that evacuation by air is a possible additional cost.

Next to treatment in a hyperbaric chamber, other possible medical emergencies SCUBA instructors may face are water aspiration (drowning), temperature related injuries (heat stroke or hypothermia, depending on your environment) and to a lesser extent hazardous marine life injuries (even a deep cut from a rock or coral could potentially lead to a complicated medical emergency).

While most of these medical emergencies are perfectly preventable, it is exactly the nature of accidents to happen when we least expect them, despite our best intentions. Carrying proper medical insurance can be a big financial risk reducer and will set your mind at ease every time you're on the job.

In addition to personal medical insurance, many insurance companies may offer coverage for your students as well. This type of coverage is particularly interesting because in the unlikely case of a training accident, it will reduce their feeling for a need to sue you to recuperate medical expenses if these expenses are automatically covered by your insurance. (more about this in the next chapter on professional liability insurance)

DAN – Divers Alert Network (www.diversalertnetwork.org) is regarded industry wide as a premium insurance provider and coverage is certainly affordable for most.

While giving numbers is always tricky and I run the risk of out-dating this book before it even hits the shelves, in 2020 a resident of (for example) the United Kingdom can obtain DAN Pro Gold insurance (the highest available coverage, which allows you to spend 365 days per year abroad) for around 300 US Dollars yearly.

 Please note that insurance is based on your country of residence and you will have to do your own research in order for you to choose the coverage that best fits your lifestyle and teaching activities.

Serious diving accidents in teaching situations are rare but you only need one to turn your entire career around so don't cheap out on medical insurance for yourself.

9.3. Professional liability insurance

On very rare occasions, despite our best intentions and greatest efforts on a daily basis, things can just go really wrong. Whether a customer dropped a tank on their own foot, the dive center's equipment had an unforeseen malfunction or you made a small mistake with big consequences, sometimes the results can be catastrophic and a lawsuit ensues.

Luckily, stories of divers suing their instructors are relatively rare compared to the vast amount of certifications that are issued worldwide but when they do happen, the costs involved can be enormous. Generally speaking, most lawsuits originate from the need for a victim to recuperate their medical expenses following a diving accident. As discussed in the previous chapter, it doesn't take much for medical emergencies to generate big bills. Having medical coverage not only for yourself but for your students may reduce the need for such a lawsuit but carrying professional liability insurance in addition to your medical insurance is still an equally wise investment.

Even when the defendant (let's say a dive instructor) is not at fault, the incurred expense of legal defense can still be massive. Liability insurance will cover such expenses and significantly reduce the stress that comes with a lawsuit. When the defendant is ruled to be at fault, the insurance company will cover the damages that need to be paid, as well.

For Europeans, the aforementioned DAN Pro Gold package may cover up to as much as 3.000.000 Euro in professional liability, next to the medical insurance coverage. For North Americans it may be worth looking at the PADI and NAUI endorsed Vicencia & Buckley for professional liability coverage. (www.diveinsurance.com)

SDI/TDI Instructors may also want to look into insurance through First Dive Insurance (www.tdisdi.com/first-dive-insurance)

SSI, NASE and RAID endorse Witherspoon & Associates (www.scubains.com)

If one day you decide to leave the diving industry or stop working as a SCUBA instructor, you should consider keeping your professional liability insurance for at least a few more years. After all, it's not unheard of for divers to sue their dive instructors many years after their training, citing errors during their initial certification course many years ago as the reason for a present-day accident.

Just like your medical insurance, I hope you will never need your liability insurance and your instructor trainer will teach you many defensive teaching techniques that will make diving accidents very unlikely. Nevertheless, get insured!

9.4. Retirement planning

Get your business shoes on. This is probably the kind of stuff you're running away from, choosing the life of a SCUBA instructor but, just like math in high school, it has to be done in order to succeed in your long term career goals.

If you're choosing to become a dive instructor, I must congratulate you. Philosophically speaking, you're already retiring and getting started on the lifestyle you truly want to live. You're a champion!

From a financial standpoint, however, if you are teaching outside of Western Europe, North America or Australia, it's very possible that you will need to take some active measures to ensure economic stability for your future. Whether you are currently 18 years old or 65, it's important to think about how you're going to make sure you won't be financially helpless when your physical abilities no longer permit you to work as a full time SCUBA instructor.

I'm not a financial advisor and you will certainly need to do additional research, based on your country of employment or residence and your personal financial situation but let's at least organize some basic ideas that could help you safeguard your future.

IRA, Independent Retirement Arrangements, would be the most obvious choice. You open an account with a financial institution of your preference and commit to setting aside a reasonable amount of your income to start saving up for the future. The biggest problem with relying solely on IRA's though, is that it's hard to predict what the eventual outcome will be. As of 2010, low savings rates, financial crises, and poor stock market performance had caused retirement savings account values to fall so low that 75% of Americans nearing retirement age had less than $30,000 in their retirement accounts.

Real estate is another interesting option. It's impossible for me to know where you, the reader, will eventually work as a SCUBA instructor. Chances are that a lot of you will be working in exotic locations around the world in the Caribbean, South East Asia or perhaps parts of Africa. If this is the case, you may want to consider putting some of your income towards acquiring real estate. I was able to obtain a small plot of land on a Caribbean island and build a house on it for the fraction of the cost of a house in Europe or North America, now allowing me to live rent-free, while building equity for the future. Of course, for those of you planning to roam the world with your new credential, this may not be an option. Also make sure that if you're buying property abroad, you surround yourself with proper legal counsel to make sure the title is clear and eventually yours.

Buying into a dive center may be another way to solidify your work into something more lasting and tangible but of course, that's a question of budget.

9.5 Run yourself as a business

We have previously discussed how in certain parts of the world the SCUBA industry is somewhat unregulated. We have also discussed the need for training, equipment, insurance, work visas, retirement plans etc. Don't let this seeming complexity of the industry discourage you. Let it encourage you to take a higher level of responsibility over your own business conduct.

In many other professions the career path is well laid out, employers cover all the insurance and retirement planning and in some jobs all you really need to do is show up and work. A successful career in SCUBA will definitely require more of you, both in the sense of career path planning and financial planning.

One way that has consistently worked for me, is to run myself as a business, even if I'm "just" an employee. What this means is that I actively keep track of the expenses that are associated with my career choice (my yearly license fee to the agency, my yearly insurance dues, my equipment expenses etc.). I also take responsibility for the fact that in most locations, nobody is doing retirement planning for me, so part of my income needs to be set aside for the long term.
Most people will take whatever salary or commission they get and spend it while "trying to save some money".

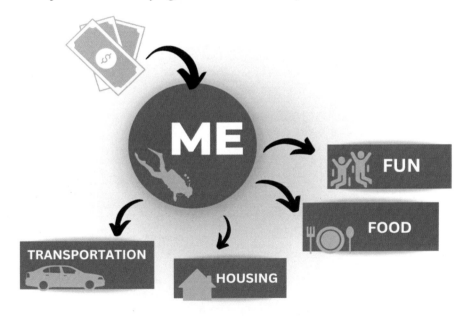

The best approach is to pinpoint how much income you need every month to survive, then make sure whatever job(s) you take on pays more than that and only pay yourself what you strictly need in order to survive. Basically, what is happening is that every dollar or euro I make doesn't go directly to me. It goes to an imaginary "ME inc." (I don't recommend you start a real corporation at first).

I work for the "Me inc." and "they" pay me a "salary" but also put money aside for my other long-term expenses so that at the end of the year, I'm covered. Everything else goes to Me inc. You can take this several steps further and compartmentalize your imaginary business, by allocating certain percentages of the income every month to long-term goals such as retirement, a stock portfolio, a real estate budget, a travel budget etc.

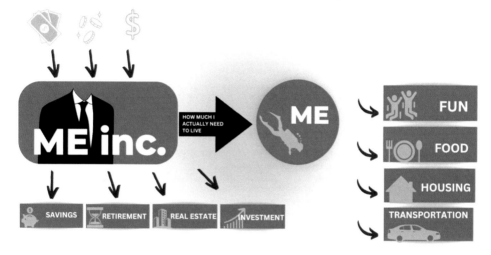

Most people's reaction to this concept is "well I don't make enough anyway so that won't work" but usually this claim is either false (they're simply used to spending whatever comes in) or they are stuck in a position that simply doesn't pay enough for what they need to properly take care of their future. Even if all you can do is structurally put 50 USD per month towards -let's say- a real estate budget, this will eventually add up and may open up opportunities in the future that are currently not even known to you. The simple act of setting up this structure and slowly starting to "grow your inc." will eventually lead to more economic stability and career longevity.

Find an app called "Revolut". They're an online financial institution and they have a very attractive system for creating what they call "vaults". You can create as many compartments inside your account as you wish, give them names and transfer as much or as little as you wish to each of them. Once the money is in the vault, it will no longer appear as part of your total balance so you can't spend it by accident.

Did You Know?

The serenity and calmness of the underwater world can have a positive effect on mental well-being, reducing stress and anxiety.

10. Finding Your Niche

To make sure your career is a lasting one that will give you all the job satisfaction and fulfillment that you were looking for when considering this new career, it's important to never stop learning and to pursue those things in diving that really get you going.

Whether it's cave diving, capturing that perfect underwater photo or teaching people who have physical challenges, find whatever it is that you are particularly passionate about and find a way to credentialize yourself so you can teach it to others.

10.1. Specializing

The most immediate way to get started on experimenting with different challenges in diving is to specialize. Most training agencies offer a broad range of continuing education options through 'Specialty Courses'. These (often shorter) programs focus on specific diving activities, using specialized equipment or diving in a specific geographical location.

It's very common for dive instructors to carry at least a few specialty instructor certifications because it obviously improves your resume and teaching opportunities, they are often not overly hard to obtain and they allow you to teach those things that you're really passionate about.

Wreck diving, deep diving, search and recovery diving and fish identification, just to name a few, are great ways to keep your own passion alive by inserting variety in your teaching options and you'll get a great thrill out of turning people onto the same activities that interest you.

 Furthermore, some specialities are simply a non-negotiable must in certain areas. Think drysuit or altitude diving. Enriched air diving is another great example of a specialty that is very popular with most divers and therefore an easy return on investment as an instructor.

10.2. Underwater photography and videography

For those divers who already have a strong interest and talent for imagery, taking that skill underwater can open the door to a whole new area of extra income potential.

Most divers and especially new dive students are prepared to pay handsomely to get their picture taken or for a small video report of their underwater adventures. For safety reasons it's not recommended that you, as a SCUBA instructor, be involved in picture taking or filming while you are teaching, but when not teaching you may want to join other instructors or dive guides and capture the adventures of their divers. You may be surprised how many divers would be willing to pay you for your service. Some dive centers and resorts hire people specifically for this job.

Many dive operations also prefer updated and beautiful content for their website, social media pages or advertising over stock footage that looks generic and somewhat fake. You could be the one providing this content.

If you have an inclination towards photography or if you are particularly skilled in videography and video editing, it may be well worth looking for additional training with an expert who can teach you the technical and artistic specifics for applying your skills underwater and producing great results.

Some ideas to get started:

- If you have limited underwater photography experience, start small. A somewhat basic point-and-shoot camera like the Olympus TG5 or similar with underwater housing is a great way to start. Once you get into full DSLR plus underwater housing, you'll quickly be spending several thousands and (probably) can't afford to accidentally flood your rig. When you're truly ready, you can always upgrade and sell your old equipment.

- Portfolio is everything. Everyone with an underwater camera can call themselves an underwater photographer but you'll need to make sure you have content to back up your claim. This content could be very handy to feed your designated

SCUBA Facebook or Instagram profile we talked about earlier. You can also start a basic website on www.wordpress.com or www.wix.com and show off your work.

- While I'm generally against working for free, the only way to truly build a portfolio is by taking pictures. A lot. The best way to do this is to offer people to join them on their dives and take shots. Make sure there's a variety of wildlife, divers, close ups etc. Experience is key.

- If you claim to be an underwater photographer, your resume better be visually stunning.

10.3. Technical diving

Technical diving refers to diving outside of the recreational no-stop limits. This means that technical divers dive profiles that don't allow direct ascents to the surface without decompression stops or they may face serious risks of decompression sickness or death.

Technical diving is a very specialized activity that requires intense training and specialized equipment and many divers, even very experienced ones, find the training challenging. This means that technical diving is not a small side project for you to beef up your resume, but rather a very specific choice that will steer your career in a certain direction.

As a new instructor and an experienced diver, you may consider taking entry-level technical training as it will make you a better deep and enriched air instructor, as well as putting you one step ahead of the students you teach.

If you are already a certified technical diver and are planning on becoming a dive instructor, the step to becoming a Tec instructor may not be as big and you may just have found your niche. Even if this is the path you have already decided on, there is great value in teaching your fair share of entry-level SCUBA courses to get some much needed experience in working with students and managing risk.

Depth and gas specifications differ between agencies but, generally speaking, most agencies consider "recreational diving" to be to a maximum depth of 40 meters or 130 feet. Beyond this point, most technical certifications start, usually still using air as a bottom gas but adding decompression stops and enriched air gasses (often 50%, 80% or 100%) to the dive plan. Most agencies consider diving on air unsafe beyond depths of 50 meters or 165 feet. It is at this point that Trimix certifications come into the mix. (Trimix is a mixture of helium, oxygen and nitrogen).

Technical diving (and especially teaching it) is not a natural progression for most dive instructors, but it's certainly a specialized career path for those who are willing to take on the added challenge, effort and cost. Be aware, too, that not all dive centers are capable of offering technical training, even if you are a certified tec instructor. The need for specialized equipment, maintenance and gas filling equipment and procedures also make this a very specialized niche.

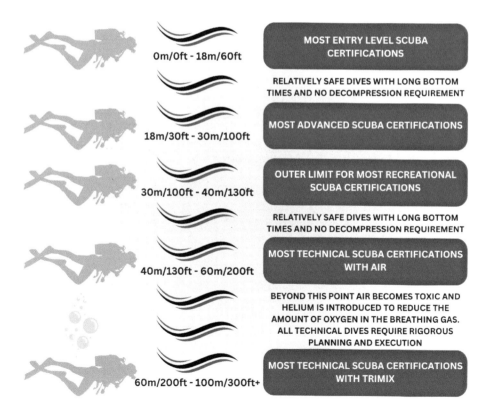

0m/0ft - 18m/60ft

MOST ENTRY LEVEL SCUBA CERTIFICATIONS

RELATIVELY SAFE DIVES WITH LONG BOTTOM TIMES AND NO DECOMPRESSION REQUIREMENT

18m/30ft - 30m/100ft

MOST ADVANCED SCUBA CERTIFICATIONS

30m/100ft - 40m/130ft

OUTER LIMIT FOR MOST RECREATIONAL SCUBA CERTIFICATIONS

RELATIVELY SAFE DIVES WITH LONG BOTTOM TIMES AND NO DECOMPRESSION REQUIREMENT

40m/130ft - 60m/200ft

MOST TECHNICAL SCUBA CERTIFICATIONS WITH AIR

BEYOND THIS POINT AIR BECOMES TOXIC AND HELIUM IS INTRODUCED TO REDUCE THE AMOUNT OF OXYGEN IN THE BREATHING GAS. ALL TECHNICAL DIVES REQUIRE RIGOROUS PLANNING AND EXECUTION

60m/200ft - 100m/300ft+

MOST TECHNICAL SCUBA CERTIFICATIONS WITH TRIMIX

10.4. Adaptive teaching

Teaching diving is immensely rewarding in itself. While seeing that smile on a newly certified diver's face is probably one of the main reasons most of us got into this profession, there is something extra special about working with people who are faced with additional challenges in life.

 Diving is not exclusively for those who are in 100% perfect physical condition and actually offers a great level of satisfaction to people who have some additional hurdles to take in daily life.

For many years, our resort has been frequented by a lovely married couple of which the woman was in a wheelchair. Getting on and off the boats and in and out of the water required a bit of team work on behalf of herself and all of the staff but almost all of my admiration went to the husband who relentlessly held on to his wife's tank valve throughout every single dive to give her that extra bit of propulsion that her webbed gloves couldn't provide in certain situations. When I asked him once if this wasn't intensely tiring, I received the answer that made me a fan of teaching people who are physically challenged: "Yes, it's definitely a little tiring, but it's all worth it to me, because when we're in the water is the only time we can still dance with each other."

There are programs in existence that will provide additional training to certified instructors to become what is commonly referred to as an 'Adaptive SCUBA Instructor'. At the College, we teach the amazing Diveheart program that trains people to become Adaptive Diver, Adaptive Buddy, Advanced Adaptive Buddy and Adaptive Instructor. It's a one week program that will forever change the way you look at diving.

When you think of physically challenged divers, your first thoughts probably run to paraplegic or maybe quadriplegic people who often need to learn additional techniques for propulsion. Other challenges that can be overcome in diving are blindness (imagine the sensation of 'weightlessness'), hearing disability (but some great underwater signaling skills) or people with learning difficulties, cognitive disabilities or post-traumatic stress disorder.

While not every adaptive class can result in certification due to certain physical limitations, participation is almost always an option if physicians can give their approval. That experience in itself can be very rewarding for both the diver and the instructor.

If you're a people person (which you almost certainly are if you're reading this book) then this extra set of skills is absolutely worth looking into. Be warned, you won't only change other people's lives but also your own.

Agencies that are worth checking out are

Diveheart - www.diveheart.org
HSA Handicapped SCUBA Association - www.hsascuba.com
IAHD International Association for Handicapped Divers - www.iahd.org

10.5. Environmental programs

As the world's reefs are more and more under threat from overfishing, oil spills, global warming and poor coastal community management, there's a great responsibility set aside for us as SCUBA instructors.

Luckily, the audience (our potential divers) are increasingly interested in learning about and understanding these threats, finding out how they can help and taking action. Eco-tourism is growing and many new and experienced divers desire to make a difference.

At the dive school I've partnered with in Utila we run a specialized three month 'Marine Conservation Instructor Development Course' to train new instructors in more than just teaching diving. They learn how to work with volunteers, set up research programs, process research data (mainly in regards to whale sharks and lionfish in our area) and local community outreach programs. This program quickly became one of our most popular packages and many of these instructors now work in research centers ranging from Indonesia to the Maldives.

Even knowing how to conduct smaller programs such as the coral bleaching surveys by Coral Watch (www.coralwatch.org) or the REEF Fish Survey Project (www.reef.org) can be very nice assets on your resume to show an employer that you have an 'eco' edge to bring to their dive center. Often, learning these programs costs nothing but time and effort.

10.6. Managing a dive center

Many of my former graduates aren't just dive instructors but have worked their way up to managing their own or someone else's dive center. If you're not interested in running an operation then this is obviously not for you, but for those with a background in management or with a healthy dose of people skills and business insight, this may add a challenging new facet to your career in the diving industry.

There is no specific training for becoming a dive operations manager and the requirements or expectations that dive center owners put forward may vary. At the dive centers I've partnered with we do offer workshops for people with this specific ambition to give them an insight into course pricing, staff management and marketing. You don't necessarily need a business degree to be able to run a dive shop but it may help and many online courses are available too to beef up your resume.

The best way to learn how to run a dive operation is simply by doing it. All it takes to get some hands-on experience is simply to be proactive and work closely with the people who run the dive center you work at. Once you've gained some experience, you may find yourself in the position of head-instructor, coordinating the planning of course schedules, coming up with new marketing initiatives or other leadership tasks.

Did You Know?

Diving with a buddy reduces your chances of getting eaten
by a shark by exactly 50%
(Kidding! Sharks are friends and SCUBA divers rarely face
negative shark encounters)

11. Becoming an Industry Leader

11.1. There is no 'I' in 'TEAM'

Like most normal businesses, the dive centers I have worked with have seen many ups and downs for a variety of reasons. I've spent a lot of time analyzing what the secret formula was for those 'ups' in hopes to replicate the circumstances and generate a situation of constant high performance.

 The true key to both individual and collective success lies in the degrees of teamwork that are happening in and around the dive center. Our collective image is only as strong as the most individualistic person on staff and a poor collective image will negatively influence even the strongest staff member.

I genuinely get a kick out of those days where everything just seems to fall into place. Invoices are being made and paid on time, student divers receive all the correct study materials at the front desk, class rooms have been tidied up before anyone intends to use them and the boat leaves on time for a smooth trip to one of our favorite dive sites after a role model boat briefing.

At the end of the day, all of these individual details that are the result of a team that works like a well-oiled machine, make all of us look like we know what we're doing because we're simply 'good at it'. This will reflect in positive online reviews, good tips from customers and a great after-work atmosphere with the colleagues. In the long run, everyone benefits from a job at a high-energy workplace that is known for its qualitative services.

I know very few high profile key members of the diving community who aren't highly skilled in team play and it is my suggestion to each individual who would like to make it big in diving to learn to work in a team. We don't all need to be head honchos, in fact, being a team player is much more than that. Whether you are a natural leader or prefer to follow someone who can give direction, your personal reputation will be highly influenced by your ability to function in a team.

COME DIVE WITH <u>ME</u> BECAUSE I OFFER

- 10 AVAILABLE HOURS PER DAY
- OPEN WATER, ADVANCED, RESCUE AND DIVEMASTER TRAINING
- NITROX, DEEP, WRECK AND NIGHT SPECIALTY COURSES
- EQUIPMENT REPAIR
- MY PERSONAL INSTRUCTIONAL STYLE

 # COME DIVE WITH <u>US</u> BECAUSE <u>WE</u> OFFER

- 60 AVAILABLE HOURS PER DAY
- OPEN WATER, ADVANCED, RESCUE AND DIVEMASTER TRAINING
- ALL SPECIALTY COURSES
- TECHNICAL DIVER TRAINING
- MARINE BIOLOGY
- EQUIPMENT REPAIR
- RECEPTIONIST, SOCIAL MEDIA PRESENCE, FAST EMAIL REPLIES
- CHOOSE WHICH INSTRUCTIONAL STYLE BEST FITS YOU

11.2. You and your employer

For the vast majority of you who aren't planning on starting their own dive business right away (that would be an entirely separate book all together) you're going to end up in a situation where a dive shop owner hires you to work for them, and that's a great opportunity in itself.

In the previous chapters, we have already discussed the importance of 'choosing' an employer that fits your personal aspirations and narrowing down the types of dive centers you want to be associated with. This choice will greatly influence who you will become as a professional diver and because of that, you should strive to develop a good working relationship with the people that operate the facilities you'll be working out of. Consider it part of the team play.

Being able to develop yourself as an instructor while working at someone's facilities is actually a wonderful opportunity. If that someone also understands and supports your personal ambitions and gives you the tools and opportunities necessary to grow, you are on a golden path to greatness. Good, hard working, long term employees are surprisingly hard to come by in this industry and being one will certainly set you apart in the eyes of your employer. Work hard to develop that relationship and you will see that a lot of mutual benefits will arise.

I've used many of my other skills to help diving businesses grow into what they are today because I was able to meet agreeable terms with the owners that were in both of our interests. If I did a (much needed) free overhaul of the website, they would acquire that new sidemount gear that I was asking for and support my training to become a sidemount instructor. The benefits should be obvious: A new, more efficient website drives more business and a new skill added to the curriculum would add income to both myself and the dive center. If we were to part ways, they would still have a great website they could keep and I would still have additional skill and teaching experience on my resume.

Over the last few years I've applied this way of thinking often when negotiating projects with dive center owners, to a point where 90% of my plans could count on instant logistical support.

This has propelled both myself and the businesses to being key players in the industry, able to offer a broad curriculum, boasting an excellent track record, having pristine and well equipped facilities and both being financially profitable.

Developing this type of relationship with your employer will take time and it's really only an option if you intend to work there long term. Developing trust and mutual respect is a slow process and both sides will need to be willing to prove themselves (you a bit more than them) and put in a reasonable amount of trust and mutual dependency so that eventually everybody can grow.

Personally, I consider this symbiosis a key ingredient to a successful career if you are not willing or able to buy and manage your own training facility.

11.3. Being a good salesperson

If you've made it this far in the book, you should have figured out by now that if you want to be successful in the dive industry then, just like any other industry, you'll have to do some sales.

Luckily, that's not a bad thing at all. 'Being a salesperson' is often associated with being a shark who's trying to get as much money out of people in exchange for some overpriced snake oil. I've got some good news: As dive instructors, we sell the stuff that dreams are made of! You're reading this very book because the idea of advancing as a diver is something that keeps you awake at night, and I wrote this book to convince you to go and chase those dreams, not because I'm an evil car salesman selling an empty box but because a diving career is a genuinely fantastic product and it needs to be 'sold' that way!

If you've taken the advice from chapter 8 to heart, then you've probably given some thought to specializing yourself after your instructor training and making it a mission to find your niche, that thing you really like and want to be really good at. Wouldn't it be an absolute shame if you went through all that effort and nobody knew the courses you offer even existed?

Most people's perception of a dive course is that it's much like a driver's license: You get certified and then you can dive. What they often don't realize is that most training agencies have an entire structure of continuing education courses that will allow them to improve their skills, engage in different diving activities and grow in their passion as a diver. It is exactly the job of a good instructor to 'teach' them on what options they have to pursue these adventures.

As an instructor, I've found that every time I acquired a new teaching credential, I was extra enthusiastic to discuss and promote these courses to divers who had often never even heard of it. I became a Full Face Mask instructor? Suddenly everyone learnt about it and many of them wanted to sign up for the program. The dive center bought some new underwater cameras, I became a Digital Underwater Photography instructor and suddenly everyone wanted to learn how to take pictures!

A good sale is simply an act of enthusiastic communication between you and the people whom you genuinely suspect may benefit from whatever it is you are selling. Whatever it is that you are excited about, you will eventually become good at. When you're good at something, people will want to learn it from you and will be willing to offer you a decent fee for whatever it is you sell, if they know it's for sale. That's exactly the sales part of your job as a SCUBA instructor.

 Your ability to make people excited about whatever it is you are offering will increase the overall number of students you can instruct, the variety of courses you can offer and eventually it will be this that makes you a key player in the dive industry.

11.4. Networking and Trade Shows

If you're looking to become an industry leader, a good network of experienced or ambitious people around you is indispensable. They will inspire you with fresh ideas, may be able to teach you new skills that improve your own curriculum and they'll have connections of their own that will help you advance your professional development.

A great way to develop an international network around you is to visit dive industry trade shows regularly. The biggest and most visited trade show in North America being DEMA (www.demashow.org) is exclusively a B2B (business to business) event, which is great for running into like-minded professionals, getting a first hand look at new technologies and attending business seminars.

Other trade shows in North America that are worth considering visiting are 'Scubashow' in Long Beach, California, 'Beneath The Sea' in New Jersey and 'Our World Underwater' in Chicago. Unlike DEMA, all of these are B2C (business to consumer) shows, open to the general public and professionals alike. They're great places to get a sense of what the average Joe diver is interested in and looking for.

In Europe, you may consider 'Birmingham Dive Show' and 'Paris Dive Show', which are both b2c shows as well.

If you have your eyes set on becoming a key player in the SCUBA industry, it's certainly worth visiting these trade shows and slowly developing your network.

11.5. Becoming an instructor trainer

While not immediately a relevant or realistic goal when first becoming a SCUBA instructor, I know that as soon as I realized what an instructor trainer was, I knew I wanted to become one.

The daily routine (if routine is at all a word that is applicable in this industry) of a trainer is very different from that of a dive instructor and less time is spent in the water comparatively. An instructor trainer is usually not only in charge of training other dive instructors, but also the general conduct of instructors on staff in a dive center. It's their responsibility to make sure courses are taught up to standards, everything is safe and that the dive center achieves its professional goals.

With most training agencies, becoming an instructor trainer is not immediately achievable for new instructors, but there are certainly things you can do early on in your career to facilitate the path towards becoming a trainer. The first and most obvious thing to do is to gain as much teaching experience as you possibly can; not just entry-level courses but a wide variety of continuing education levels.

Speaking of continuing education, another thing you can do is to continuously look to improve your own skills and make sure you're a well rounded instructor, as discussed in previous chapters.

Lastly, if you're looking to become an instructor trainer it's probably smart to start thinking long-term. The most successful trainers I know don't roam around but have a solid working relationship with one or two dive schools, and they market and organize their programs from there. Find a place that has potential and be actively involved in its growth and success.

Did You Know?

In tropical water, the average diver burns 300 calories per hour of diving. This can increase to as much as 600 calories per hour in colder water.

12. The 20% Rule

In chapter one of this book we talked about 'dedication' and how persistence will create longevity and longevity will quickly place you within the 20% of SCUBA instructors who 'make it'. I think that it is only fitting that we end this book with a chapter on exactly that. How do we get in that 20% club?

12.1. Longevity

Not an IDC goes by where one of my candidates wasn't Open Water certified by someone I trained. If that's not the case, at least someone ended up in my class by the referral of someone I trained previously. This isn't because I am some kind of incredible SCUBA god that everyone refers candidates to. In fact, most somewhat active PADI Course Directors will probably tell you the same thing. It's simply the result of industry longevity.

As we discussed in the first chapter, about 80% of instructors don't renew their teaching credential after just two years. Some by design because they embarked on a gap year and did exactly that, some because they just wanted to taste the IDC experience and some because they couldn't find a formula that worked for them. At first glance a sad statistic for sure, but upon deeper inspection a welcome trend for those who are serious about this line of work but are intimidated by the amount of people who try to enter it every year.

Don't get me wrong, this is not about some weird kind of schadenfreude about people whose dreams didn't pan out the way they were supposed to. It's about seeing the massive silver lining on a statistic that may seem intimidating if you instinctively count yourself in the 80% that quit, but is quite the opportunity if you count yourself in the 20% that persists.

The key is to stick with it. As with any line of work, you tend to enter the industry as a 'junior'. Even if you are a certified instructor, and even if you (against my advice) acquired every possible instructor credential under the sun before starting your first job, there is rarely a path that doesn't first go straight through a trial by fire. When working in a team, new instructors rarely get first pick on which courses they want to teach. Much less do they get dibs on the really big and profitable courses (nor should they be teaching big courses considering the limited experience they have). In most dive centers the senior staff will end up with the better deals and that's just the way it is. This is not some sadistic quirk of the diving industry. It makes perfect sense to award some privileges to more experienced staff, especially if they've shown to be willing to stick around. Remember though: only two years...

12.2. Gaining SuperPowers

Another way it can gradually become easier to optimize your income, as we've discussed before, is to gain additional teaching credentials and get specialized. It's important to note, however, that the newly certified instructor who loaded up on an ungodly amount of technical diver and specialty instructor credentials is hardly more employable than the one who didn't.

Yes, I know, earlier I recommended you specialize. But only somewhat! A blank CV with the bare minimum credentials is indeed a tough proposition to compete with other newly certified instructors and most dive centers will likely prefer to hire a new instructor who can also teach a nitrox or deep specialty here and there. So getting some specialized credentials from the onset is indeed a good idea, but don't overdo it.

I regularly get inquiries for divers who want to spice up their IDC by adding specialty instructor training, IDC Staff instructor training, Tec instructor training and a full Trimix diver certifications. I'm not exaggerating. More often than not, I actually have to 'unsell' them on these ideas. Specializing early on is good, and I understand that you want to give this everything you've got from the onset. However, overdoing it is often a blood red flag for dive center owners when inspecting a CV. Most dive center managers simply aren't looking for newly certified instructors who went all the way to the highest conceivable level of certification with the bare minimum of actual experience under their belt.

Finding your niche and adding more (and often more lucrative) credentials to your portfolio or 'gaining more superpowers' as I like to call it, is an amazing thing that should be allowed to happen naturally as you progress through your career. Let's face it: what does an IDC Staff Instructor with the bare minimum 25 certifications and mere weeks of teaching experience under their belt truly have to offer to new IDC candidates? Should someone straight out of IDC really be teaching technical diving with only the bare minimum of difficult and unpredictable Open Water students to draw lessons from? While I agree that 'age' or 'longevity' by themselves are poor metrics to judge an instructor by, experience is key and can't be bought.

If I just turned your smile upside down and you're thinking "damn, that's me. I wanted to get into this to teach Tec and get there sooner than later" don't let this discourage you. But take a breath. Smell the roses. The process may be long but the road to your destination is far more important than the destination itself. I've enjoyed every single Open Water course I've taught and each one of those students have brought me closer to the Trimix Instructor Trainer credential and all the other bells and whistles on my CV today. The system works but it simply takes time to get there.

You'd be surprised how quickly two years go by when you're doing something you love.

12.3. Who Are The 20%?

The 20% now may seem some secretive society of SCUBA instructors who all know each other. A SCUBA Illuminati if you will..

I will once again have to disappoint you. Yes, names start looking very familiar, you'll make more SCUBA friends and 'frienemies' and many of us regularly bump into one another. When faced with a student who needs a referral to a location I don't service, I'm likely to recommend one of those familiar names. New students often choose us 'because they've heard of us'. But as far as our secret SCUBA society goes, that's about it.

The point of the 20% club is that it's much more a designator of longevity than of group size. It's overwhelmingly clear that getting across that two-year-gap seems to be one of the biggest indicators of industry success. Likely this is because most of us can't make it past the gap without passion, dedication and hard work. Besides the lucky few who've had disproportionate outside support, everyone who made it across the two-year-gap had to find a way to make it work.

Again, I'm not trying to glorify some sort of excessive hustle-culture or promote burnouts. In fact, one of the first things we discussed in this book is that my personal definition of success is a state of emotional and financial balance and well-being while having the freedom to pursue your passions.

And so we are about to conclude my contributions to this book. I hope it can serve as a field guide for those of you who are about to embark on the mission of a lifetime. Allow me to wish you success and longevity. Stay safe and stay happy.

Advice
and Stories
from the Pros

13. Advice and Stories from the Pros

In this chapter I'm going to give the word to some of the many successful PADI professionals in my circle. I gave them some basic guidelines for writing this, but other than that, this is unedited content with their real-life experiences and advice.

Tom St George, Cave Diver, Diving Journalist and Professional Underwater Photographer - Mexico

I started scuba diving when I emigrated from the UK to New Zealand at age 30. I was already looking for a change, having become sick of the 'rat race' of working in London as a web developer and looking for a better work/life balance. Living in New Zealand I worked as a senior Web Developer at a digital media agency. On the weekends I would go snowboarding in the winter and scuba diving for the rest of the year. After about 8 years in New Zealand, the wanderlust struck and I decided I wanted to travel and see more of the world, and dive some new places, and so I started traveling South East Asia for diving and supporting myself with freelance web development work. By this point I had trained up to the Rescue Diver level.

I met my partner Julia when diving in Pulau Weh, Indonesia. She was heading to Mabul in Malaysia to work a season as a divemaster, and so I went there with her. I actually only did my Divemaster course because it was cheaper to do the DMT than to stay there for a season as a paying customer. I did enjoy my Divemaster training and also finishing the season working as a Divemaster, but that was the only time I worked as a DM. However, it was diving in Mabul and getting to know the dive sites well that re-ignited my passion for photography and specifically underwater photography. At that point I was just using an old compact camera and homemade video light and shooting macro. After some more traveling around South East Asia, we decided to travel to Mexico to undertake cave diving training. We fell in love with the cenotes and when I started taking pictures here, it eventually led to my new career as an underwater photographer.

My friends and family were very supportive of my travel and

becoming a scuba diver. They were initially less supportive about becoming a cave diver. They now realize that despite how it is sometimes portrayed in the media, it is really an 'extreme' sport and with the correct training and equipment it is actually very safe. Everyone has been very supportive of my switch to being a full-time underwater photographer and my attempt to 'live the dream' so to speak.

I am an underwater photographer, underwater photography instructor, and dive journalist. My work involves both private photoshoots for divers and commercial work for brands. I have been lucky enough to work for some big names such as PADI, SSI, Mares, Apeks, Hollis, OTS etc. and I'm also extremely lucky in that I get to do a few interesting trips a year, writing articles for some of the UK dive magazines. On top of that, I get to teach workshops on underwater photography which I really enjoy. In my spare time, I get to work on my cave diving and cenote photography.

I think the highlight of my career so far was being a runner up for the Underwater Photographer of the Year 2017 in the wide-angle category. It was also a big honor to be asked to co-host a cave and cavern diving photography workshop with WetPixel.

I don't think I could ever go back to working in an office again. Although I still end up spending a lot more time on the computer editing than I do actually diving, I get to set my own hours and work from home (or anywhere really). Diving has made a huge impact on my life. When I moved to New Zealand I quickly fell in love with scuba diving, and then I met my partner Julia which diving, and finally it has taken me all over the world and given me a chance to experience many adventures and make lots of memories.

My advice is just to get out there and dive as much as possible. Try new experiences and try to learn from everyone you work with as you never know what opportunities may arise and where they might lead you - keep your heart and mind open! Everyone I have met in the dive industry who is successful over the long term is very passionate about what they do. You really need to be able to find enjoyment in what you do if you want to make a career of it. Keep learning and keep developing your skills.

Renata Bonfa, PADI Course Director - Brasil

I was working in the tourism industry in Barcelona as a receptionist in a big fancy hotel, and doing night shifts to save money to go on long trips. I was pretty much a city girl. In summer I would go to the beach pretty much everyday, and would travel every time I got an opportunity. Work was just a means to an end for me.

I went on a sabbatical trip to southeast Asia, because I needed a change, and decided to quit my job and go for a 3 month trip. At some point in Thailand, I met people that had a great time on an island doing their SCUBA courses, and decided to go there and do the same. Once there and involved with the diving community there I just didn't want to leave at all, and managed to convince the school there to let me stay and work at the office for them in exchange for a Divemaster course. The rest is history, one year later I did my instructor.

The reason why I became a scuba professional is because I saw a life that was simple but Rich. I realized that that was what I wanted for myself, so I pursued it. My family doesn't understand much about SCUBA diving and generally they have no idea what it is that I actually do, but they don't oppose it either as I do have a history to be the "different" one in the family. My friends in Barcelona would tell me I have never looked happier and supported me, even though they didn't necessarily understand what I was doing. I met beautiful people in the diving industry and made great connections that serve as motivation and support to this day.

Right now, I'm a PADI Course Director, which means I train other SCUBA instructors. I think being goal oriented is ultimately what brought me here. I knew I would never want to work in any other industry ever again, so I needed to make my diving career work in terms of stability and money. I needed it to be a real job and not just a phase. And although I was not

141

looking for a job as a Course Director, I was looking for growing opportunities after doing seasons for a while. Then I sent a CV in to a dive center looking for someone who wanted to be a Staff Instructor and maybe continue as a CD. I was offered the job and took it, not really knowing if that was the way forward.

I remember telling the manager of the shop I was working at the time in Dahab about it, and her telling me "I have no doubt that you will be a Course Director in less than five years". I laughed it off and we made it a joke and called it 'my five year plan'. When less than two years later I did become a CD, she was one of the first ones to congratulate me saying "Of course your five year plan was not even a two year plan!"

To me, my biggest professional success is simply in the way I completely changed my life, from unhappy in the city with a crappy job to I love what I do everyday. Thanks to SCUBA diving I am a lot healthier I think. I barely drink anymore, I enjoy the daylight a lot more, I am more connected to nature. It's silly, but as a woman, I have learned to love my natural physical appearance a lot more too. We are always wet and messy in this industry, we have to be on good terms with our appearance. When living in the city I would never leave home without make-up on and my hair done. Now I am who I am and don't worry too much about what that looks like. All while being able to live in beautiful places I would have never imagined to even visit.

Yes, I did have to leave the industry at some short periods. Either was because I wanted to do another scuba diving course that would cost me real money (like the Instructor course). I went back to working in tourism in Barcelona for a bit so I could afford it, as my Divemaster salary in Thailand would not cover that cost. And I did have to leave it for a bit during COVID as well, which was probably the hardest thing, being scared that the world would never be the same again, and my goal was just falling apart. But I always knew I wanted in again, and managed to not give up.

If this is what you want, make a plan, and go for it! It's not always going to be easy. The mornings are early and the days might be long, but if your heart's in it, you will feel fulfilled at the end of the day.

Understand that there are different types of diving professionals. There's the ones that are doing it for just a little while, to travel and meet people, maybe as a gap year thing. They likely will not last in the industry, they will probably leave it complaining. And there are people who have decided to look at it as a real career, and they will invest in their diving education, and they will work hard to improve themselves and gain better positions in the industry. You have to decide who you want to be. To make it and become successful in the industry you have to take it seriously and not as a vacation job, that's the only way.

Yes, living in paradise islands, summer all year round is great and a privilege of our jobs, but you are not on holidays, this is your life and your job, act like it, and there will be results.

In the years preceding my first SCUBA experience I worked as an Intelligence Officer for a department of Government where I specialised in investigating cases of identity fraud. I was offered this opportunity out of College, where I primarily studied Sport Science/coaching and criminal psychology, so the offer of employment was far removed from what I thought I was preparing for, but an interesting one nonetheless. Alongside my brother in 2003 at age 25, I embarked on a sabbatical backpacking trip around Australia which is where I was certified as a PADI Open Water diver. During our training course in Cairns, we completed our certification dives on the Great Barrier Reef and returned numerous times post-certification to enjoy this natural wonder.

After around two and a half years on returning to the U.K an unwanted and unforeseen change in personal circumstance was forced upon me. Within days I had emailed a dive centre in New Zealand, obtained a working holiday visa and booked a flight having made the decision to remove myself from what I viewed as a toxic environment. I moved to New Zealand in 2006 to work at Dive Wellington and complete a professional internship where I was subsequently certified Advanced Open Water through to Divemaster before extending my stay to complete my instructor course and MSDT in April 2007. I made the decision to become an instructor because after my certification as a Divemaster I was used by my dive centre to actively assist on courses and to complete Divemaster conducted programs. As I progressed and got more involved in the mentoring and instructional process, I found an immense satisfaction in helping others achieve their goals so I sought the chance to have a greater influence which ultimately led to instructor certification. So, it was the teaching and mentoring aspect that first attracted me to pursue a career and 'SCUBA' was the vehicle that would allow me to achieve it.

The love of diving which I now have was something that, for me, developed soon after I realised the position I was now in. During this time my family were fully supportive and encouraging of my pursuit of becoming a professional diver. It takes a genuine support structure to help you achieve your goals, even when those goals are likely to keep you away from loved ones for extended periods. I was, and still am lucky to continue to receive the same encouragement which has allowed me to progress to where I now find myself. Today I hold the rating of PADI Platinum Course Director. My other senior credentials include Emergency First Response Instructor Trainer, Tec Instructor Trainer and licensed Boat Captain. I got to where I am not only because of the aforementioned family support, but through a lot of dedication towards continual self improvement coupled with a passion for the industry I am involved in and the encouragement and mentorships of fellow professionals whose advice and guidance have been invaluable.

Being certified as a PADI Course Director was a special moment in my life, not just my diving career and although many would believe or assume that is an obvious statement, I can say with complete honesty that the evening I completed my Divemaster course was on-par with the feeling of pride and success. I was fortunate that my speculative email to a dive centre in New Zealand all those years ago struck a chord with the reader. I met my boss on my second day in New Zealand and developed an instant admiration of him. He pulled up on his motorcycle, took off his riding jacket revealing arms covered in Maori tattoos, took me next door for a coffee and spoke to me about what was expected of me and how we would get me where I wanted to be. He didn't say it at the time (probably because it might not have meant anything) but he was also a Course Director. 10 years after this moment, I was a motorcycle riding, coffee drinking Course Director with arms of Maori tattoos who cares about his students excelling, the moral being; never underestimate the positive influence you can have on a person. How you treat someone in a single moment can change the course of their life. I will be thankful every day of my life for having met Dave Drane. Diving didn't contribute to my life as much as it gave me a life. For 17 years (as of this revision) I've lived and worked in various countries across the world. I've seen and experienced things I'd never have known existed and met some truly amazing people along the way. I heard once that 'travel is the only thing that costs money but makes you richer', diving has been the vessel that has allowed me to experience this first hand and consent to its accuracy.

My advice to aspiring professionals would be to allow yourself to be absorbed in the process, to be an active part of the learning in order to get the most out of it. Have trust and faith in your mentor or instructor as they have been through the same system you wish to be a part of so use their experiences for your own growth. Success is just an inevitable byproduct of having a great attitude and applying yourself. By being prepared, organised, dedicated and by listening to your peers and applying yourself then you are setting yourself up for success. All divers have a passion for being underwater, but as a pro we need to project that enthusiasm into our teaching and our interactions with other divers in the hope of inspiring them, then it will lead us on the path to professional success.

Abigail Smith, Marine Conservationist - Australia

I was 16 years old when I first went diving during a family holiday to Sharm El Sheikh, Egypt, in 2011. Both my Dad and older brother were already certified divers, and not wanting to feel left out, I decided to complete my Open Water course whilst they began working towards their Advanced certification. Still today, I always feel extremely grateful to my parents for giving me the opportunity to try out diving. I had always been drawn to water, so being underwater came relatively naturally.

Growing up in England away from the coast, scuba diving wasn't always on my radar. In fact, all throughout school I aspired to work in the film industry – behind the camera. I loved analyzing both films & novels and creating my own short productions, which is why ultimately I decided to pursue an English Literature & Film Studies degree. I've always had a keen eye for storytelling through a lens and spent many of my school holidays gaining work experience for film companies.

When I was 18 I decided to defer my university start date by a year so I could go backpacking around Australia. Fast forward three years to the final year of my studies, that urge to travel returned and it felt stronger than ever. Maybe instead of going straight into work after graduation, I could take a month to go abroad?

I remember taking a short break from writing my dissertation and started to curiously browse 'overseas internships' online. I knew that I wanted to visit a new country, ideally find an educational internship, and be in or around the water. Hours later, I had officially applied for a marine conservation internship at the Whale Shark & Oceanic Research Center (WSORC) on the island of Utila, Honduras. Looking back now, it's funny to recognize how the majority of 'big' life choices I've made also tend to follow that similar impulsive pattern...

It's safe to say that my attempt to stifle that travel bug positively failed. The short story is that my hopes of satisfying those vagabond urges by completing a month-long internship resulted in me living in Honduras for six years, from 2016 to 2022.

A week into my internship I knew I wanted to extend my stay to do my PADI Divemaster course. It was the first time I felt truly grounded. I had traveled to this tiny island alone, and suddenly found myself surrounded by people on the same page as me. Something just clicked, and I called my parents to tell them I wasn't coming home. I felt an immense sense of pride in myself for making that choice. I still do!

Not long afterwards, the school I trained with (Bay Islands College of Diving) offered me a Divemaster position on the team. I told myself that I would indulge in this lifestyle for six more months, then return home back to what I deemed to be 'reality'. But then, as you may have guessed, my dear friend and course director Nick Derutter inspired me to become a dive instructor, and then not long after that I progressed onto IDC staff instructor. That's when working in diving no longer seemed like an impractical or unreliable path, but rather a serious career. Nick is literally living proof that you can achieve the greatest success in your field without forfeiting the most adventurous and thrilling opportunities in life.

Understandably, my parents were concerned about the longevity and stability of pursuing a career in diving. Having them come visit and see me in my element made a big difference to their perspective. This provided them with a deeper understanding of not only what I do, but why I wanted to do it. Now, almost 8 years into my diving career, they are very proud of my achievements. I think whilst we all suffer the emotional repercussions of me living away from home, they respect me for going after what makes me happy in life.

For the last year I have been managing a start-up dive operation in Western Australia, in an area that has been on my bucket list for as long as I can remember: The Ningaloo Reef. Building this new business from scratch, I have been involved in every development process along with the owner and co-manager, my partner.

After working as an instructor at The College of Diving on Utila for a few years, teaching both recreational and professional courses, at the end of 2018 I was presented with an opportunity to become Program Manager of WSORC, the same NGO where it all began. I was hesitant to accept the role as I doubted my abilities to run the internship program without having a marine science degree. I compared myself to the prior managers I had met and felt an overwhelming sense of imposter syndrome. And you know what? It was the best career choice I ever made. I found my niche and built an incredible team. We taught a high quality curriculum that we wrote and mentored interns from all over the world and of all ages, providing hundreds of aspiring conservationists the tools to further their passions. By the time I said goodbye to my small island home, I had really proved myself wrong. I am, once again, immensely proud of the person I grew into during my time there.

The managerial skills, hands-on field experience, and extensive knowledge of both PADI curriculum and dive center business I gained across those years is what equipped me for my current role today.

I'm hoping that if Nick writes a third edition of this book then I can say that the greatest personal and professional success in my life as a scuba diver is owning my own company.

To date, I'd consider my greatest success to be my unwavering work ethic, rather than a specific standalone moment or occasion. As for most people working in diving, the years during and following the pandemic were challenging. My career was on standstill and I feel like I'm still trying to play catchup from those setbacks.

I absolutely relished the adventures I chased throughout my 20's. Moving countries, traveling, climbing the career ladder and investing a nauseating amount of money into my goals. But I'm starting to crave a more stable foundation in life. It would be nice to not always pack up my life every six to twelve months. To have a guest room where friends and family can visit. To rescue a dog!

I think how one person measures success can vary drastically between another. Having been trained at such a prestigious dive center, for a long time I viewed being successful in the dive industry as having a superior role at an establishment that teaches PADI professionals, offers TEC courses, internship programs, a vast range of specialties etc. But now having ventured further afield, I've witnessed how success in the dive industry can take shape in many different ways. It could look like running a smaller operation that offers snorkel tours and whale watching excursions as well as diving. It may not be 100% diving, but it's relative to the tourism opportunities in that region. Or maybe working for a dive business in a city where the diving isn't as mind blowing, but the job is secure and you could be on an attractive salary where instead you go on incredible dive trips. I've learnt that the dive industry is so much more versatile than I first perceived it to be. There's endless opportunities if you're willing to do the research and take the leap.

As the saying goes, you should 'work to live' opposed to 'live to work', but discovering a career in diving has molded every aspect of my life. Quite simply, it has given me my purpose. I met my partner through diving. My most cherished friendships have formed through our shared love for it, it's enabled me to see more of the world and become a version of myself that would never have been achievable otherwise.

To many who aspire to become a dive professional, the road can seem overwhelming. It's hard work, but that's what makes the finish line even more rewarding. You need to invest in this journey, and I've lost count of the times I've been told how "lucky" I am to be doing what I do. But it has nothing to do with luck. I worked in hospitality and saved all throughout school and university so I could afford to travel and pay for my dive certifications. I made the ballsy decision to not go home and instead take a chance on this life. I've put in a ton of work and have taken risks that haven't worked out, but I've learnt from them. This career is a possibility to everyone, as long as you really want it.

It's tricky to advise an individual on how to achieve success, as once again it depends on how you measure it. Personally, I have found that as long as I'm making myself proud, I'm succeeding in life. I know that being sedentary in life affects me massively, and the times I've been at my lowest are when I feel like I'm not progressing. I'm driven by growth and setting myself goals, and that helps me feel successful when I notice a change.

Another piece of advice that I could have used at a certain time, is try not to be intimidated by people around you who appear to know it all. The diving and marine conservation community can appear huge, but it's actually pretty small. There are a lot of big fish occupying space in small ponds, and in actual fact, they are not dominating the scene. They don't leave room or opportunity for others to progress, so why would you want to be in their pond anyway? Pay more attention to the role models who meet you with kindness and humility, because they recognize that everyone starts off in the same place.

Lastly, if like me, you're worried about not having 'the right' degree, and you're hesitant to take a risk on applying for a certain role, then I'm proof that you can. I still make plenty of mistakes, but being approachable to others and building trust with students and colleagues will get you further. I acquired all of my accolades through practical experience, through making reliable contacts and through translating what I learn to diverse audiences. For example, I have found that not everyone understands scientific or diving terminology, so communicating a concept that people can grasp is essential. This not only applies to students, but also to communities, investors, even your friends and family. At long last my degree is proving to be useful!

If you can identify your unique qualities and figure out how best to apply them, then you will become a big fish in a big ocean, and I think there's no better place to be.

Rich Synowiec, Course Director, Rebreather Instructor Trainer and owner of multiple dive shops - Michigan, USA

When I was about 9 years old I became a scuba diver. My mom, a marine biologist at the time, took the time to show me the rudimentary basics of the dive system and how to equalize and breathe underwater. When I was 19, I needed a "job." I was in college at the Center for Creative Studies in Detroit, Michigan and I had a neighbor who gave me a good reference and I started in the industry. I became a "Stock boy" at the dive shop where my parents and I got certified. Over the next year I worked my way up the PADI ladder becoming an Advanced Open Water, Rescue and then Divemaster. I was an NASDS Instructor Candidate when my buddy talked me into switching to PADI and then taking My IDC. I was 21 years Old.

My parents were all for it, as long as it was something I would use to get my college degree and move on to a more professional career. Looking back over the decades, they were of the belief that no one in the "Skilled trades" could make a living as well as someone with a college degree. I'm now in my fifties and I think they still believe I will someday get a "Real Job."

I am a PADI Course Director, PADI Trimix Instructor Trainer, PADI Tec 60 CCR Instructor on the Prism 2, PADI EFR Instructor Trainer, DAN Instructor Trainer, owner of Divers Incorporated – Ann Arbor, Divers Incorporated – White Star Quarry, owner of Scubacrap.com, and diverswebstore.com.

I think the big turning points in my life were the day I became a PADI Instructor, the day I became a Master Instructor, the day I got married, the day I became a tec trimix diver, the day I bought Divers Incorporated, the day I certified my wife Jill, The day I became a Trimix Instructor, the day I became a father of twin girls, The day I became a CCR Diver, The day I became a CCR Instructor, The day I became a Course Director, and the day I realized that I was now one of the "old guard" in the SCUBA industry.

On the evening of the day we found out we were going to have twins, I asked my wife if I should give up diving and go back to my "normal Job." You see, I took a substantial pay cut to become a dive shop owner. The potential for more was there but it was seen as a HUGE risk. My wife's response.... " Oh, Hell no... you are Way Happier Now!"

The "Risk" part of my career is something I would like to take the liberty of expanding upon. When I bought the dive shop, diving and the selling of dive equipment were the only two things I knew for certain that I was excellent at. I quit three jobs to start my dive shop. The big question my wife and I got was "aren't you scared?" The thing is, you could lose your current job tomorrow without any warning. As an owner of a dive business, you can see that coming a long way away and do something about it.

The advice that I would give would not be what most aspiring dive professionals want to hear. There is SO much negativity in our profession. Even as far as five years after I owned my dive shop, my parents would ask me "when will you get a 'real job?'"

Here are probably my key pieces of advice for aspiring dive professionals..

1. Treat Diving as a profession - You teach people how to breathe underwater. How cool is that? You should never undervalue that. You should be able to make a living teaching scuba, but it will take a lot of work on your part to make it happen. Make sure you are committed to your professional development as a business owner as well as a dive pro. Avoid the trap of working for air fills, diving privileges, discounts etc.... You can make a good living as a dive professional.

2. Find a Niche - Every Tom, Dick, Harry and Jane who want to become dive pros can be dive pros, most will wash out as a career and spend the rest of their life on Facebook telling people "The only way to make a million dollars as a dive pro is to start with two million" Of all the people in the dive industry, 80% of the people are at this level, while 20% are making enough money to raise a family, have vacations and own a home. This is true in absolutely EVERY Profession on the planet. Diving is no exception. You get out of it what you plan to put into it. If you find a niche, something that you can be good at and better at than someone else in the profession, exploit it. For some, it is looking good diving, for others it may be to travel to exotic, hard

to reach destinations, or maybe you are a tech diver who can teach tech diving... whatever it is, focus on that at first. Remember to be flexible. If it is not working, change.

3. Figure out what is important to you – If making a Million dollars out of the gate is important to you, diving is not the place to start. If having a job that pays the bills and keeps you relaxed and sane, this may be the closest to heaven for you. I made WAY more money in a career that was not even remotely related to diving. I thought "I can make enough money to go on trips" I do not have to be a dive pro. I am WAY happier as a dive pro.

4. Do Not undervalue what you do - This is probably the one that should be the first. In a world where most dive pros are discounting to get students, you need to be the one that charges the most and then gives more to your clients than they expect. Think of it as picking a brain surgeon. Do you really want to go to the lowest priced one if your life was on the line? Take the time to make sure you are charging what you need to make a living and then deliver a value that exceeds what is being paid. I can promise you, you will get a high quality student, a person you can afford to teach properly and a dive buddy who will continue to take classes from you.

5. Start out working for a dive center - Striking out on your own can be WAY more challenging than working for a dive center but there are risks in both. Working for a dive center can get you more students but they typically pay less. The value that an instructor has to a dive center lies in how they promote con ed, promote equipment sales, promote travel and how they keep people scuba diving. Make sure you are doing something work getting paid a lot for, then make sure you are getting compensated accordingly. (Revisit #4)

6. Be in the business of Diving - This is something I am pretty passionate about. As a PADI Course Director I have had to compete with other organizations that offer a cheaper course than I do. The thing is, ANYONE CAN BE A DIVE INSTRUCTOR! It does not take all that much. You can take a course from almost anywhere and earn the certification. The difference is the commitment to making it a business. There are Instructor courses out there that teach you only how to pass the test. They are typically cheaper, do not require you to purchase

new materials, do not show you how to price a course or how to teach beyond beginners. They focus on the courses you can teach rather than the bigger picture of selling the product that is YOU! Successful instructors know that diving is a business that requires more than just teaching people to dive. We sell equipment, experiences, a focus on the environment and the whole gambit of continuing education.

7. Become a Sales Pro as well as a dive pro – This will make all the difference. Remember, your first product is YOU! You need to be able to sell yourself without degrading others. You need to focus on being a sales professional as well as a dive professional.

The value of being a dive pro is making sure that when people think of diving, they think of you. Remember, everything we do counts. If we do our jobs right and people have a good time diving, they think of us. If we do not do our jobs diving and people do not have a good time diving, they also think of us. You have the choice and the power to make a difference.

To be successful as a dive instructor you need to simply teach divers you would be proud to dive with.

APPENDIX

Certification types per training organization

PADI – The Professional Association of Diving Instructors (www.padi.com)

- PADI is by far the agency with the largest market share, represented in over 180 countries and territories across the globe which creates plenty of opportunities for new PADI Open Water Scuba Instructors.
- PADI certifies the vast majority of diving instructors and the credential doesn't necessarily set you apart from the others unless you're willing to specialize.
- PADI Instructors don't need to be affiliated with a dive center or resort. While this is the preferred method for teaching courses, independent instructors can teach courses up to Divemaster, as long as they use the appropriate system and materials.

Slogan: "The Way the World Learns to Dive"

Recreational diving

- Seal Team
- Bubble Maker
- Skin Diver
- Junior Scuba Diver
- Scuba Diver (sub certifiction)
- Junior Open Water Diver
- Open Water Diver
- Advanced Open Water Diver
- Rescue Diver
- Master Scuba Diver

Specialty Courses

- Adaptive Support Diver / Adaptive Techniques
- Altitude Diver
- AWARE Specialty Diver
- Boat Diver
- Cavern Diver
- Deep Diver
- Digital Underwater Photographer

- Diver Propulsion Vehicle
- Drift Diver
- Dry Suit
- DSMB Diver
- Emergency Oxygen Provider Course
- Enriched Air Diver
- Fish Identification
- Full Face Mask Diver
- Ice Diver
- Night Diver
- Peak Performance Buoyancy
- Project AWARE
- Search and Recovery
- Rebreather Diver
- Advanced Rebreather
- Self Reliant Diver
- Sidemount Diver
- Underwater Naturalist
- Underwater Navigator
- Underwater Videographer
- Wreck Diver

Professional Courses

- Divemaster
- Assistant Instructor
- Open Water Scuba Instructor (OWSI)
- Specialty Instructor
- Master Scuba Diver Trainer (MSDT)
- IDC Staff Instructor
- Master Instructor
- PADI Course Director

Technical Courses

- Tec Basics
- Tec 40
- Tec 40 Trimix
- Tec 45
- Tec 45 Trimix
- Tec 50
- Tec 50 Trimix
- Tec Trimix 65

- Tec Trimix Diver
- Tec 40 CCR
- Tec 60 CCR
- Tec 100 CCR
- Tec CCR

NAUI - National Association of Underwater Instructors (www.naui.org)

- NAUI, founded in the United States in 1959, is the oldest diver training agency and is a non-profit organization.
The NAUI ICC (Instructor Certification Course) became the first course to make diver certification available worldwide and internationally.
- NAUI has some high profile members, starting with Jacques-Yves Cousteau all the way to Kevin Costner and Cameron Diaz and likes to advertise this fact.

Slogan: "Diver Safety Through Education".

Recreational courses

- Junior Skindiver
- Junior Scuba Diver
- Junior Advanced Scuba Diver
- Skin Diver
- Scuba Diver
- Experienced Scuba Diver
- Advanced Scuba Diver
- Master Scuba Diver

Specialty courses

- Deep Diver
- Dry Suit Diver
- Enriched Air Nitrox (EAN)Diver
- Scuba Rescue Diver
- Search and Recovery Diver
- Training Assistant
- Underwater Archaeologist
- Underwater Ecologist
- Underwater Environment
- Underwater Photographer

- Underwater Hunter and Collector
- Wreck Diver (External Survey)

Leadership courses

- Assistant Instructor
- Skin Diving Instructor
- Divemaster
- Instructor Preparation Course
- Instructor
- Instructor Trainer
- Course Director

Technical courses

- Cave Diver (Levels I, II, and III)
- Cavern Diver
- CCR Mixcd Gas Diver
- Closed Circuit Rebreather Diver
- Decompression Technique
- Heliair Diver
- Helitrox Diver
- Ice Diver
- Introduction to Technical Diving
- Mixed Gas Blender and O2 Service Technician
- Semi-closed Rebreather Diver
- Technical Nitrox Diver
- Technical Support Leader
- Technical Wreck Penetration Diver
- Tri-Mix Diver (Levels I & II)
- Wreck Penetration Diver

SSI - Scuba Schools International (www.divessi.com)

- Founded in 1970, a key difference with most other agencies is that SSI instructors can only teach courses through an SSI dive center.
- A very broad range of continuing education courses and "XR - Extended Range" Technical courses.

Slogan: "Comfort Through Repetition"

Recreational Courses

- Indoor Diver
- Junior Scuba Diver
- Scuba Diver
- Junior Open Water Diver
- Open Water Diver
- Advanced Adventure Diver
- Specialty Diver
- Advanced Open Water Diver
- Diver Stress & Rescue
- Master Diver

Specialty Courses

- Altitude diver
- Boat diving
- Deep diving
- Underwater photography
- Diver stress and rescue
- Dry suit diving
- EAN Nitrox
- Equipment techniques
- Navigation
- Night and limited visibility
- Perfect buoyancy
- Recreational sidemount diving
- River diving
- Science of diving
- Search and recovery
- Shark ecology
- Waves, tides and currents
- Wreck diving

Professional Courses

- Dive Guide (DG)
- Divemaster (DM = DG + Science of Diving)
- Snorkel Instructor
- Dive Control Specialist (DCS = DM + Snorkel instr. + Diving assistant instr.)
- Training Specialist (TS = DCS + limited specialties instructor)
- Open Water Instructor (OWI)
- Classified Open Water Instructor
- Specialty Instructor (SI = OWI + 2 specialties instr.)
- Advanced Open Water Instructor (AOWI = OWI + 4 specialties)
- Divemaster Instructor (DMI = AOWI + online exam)
- Dive Control Specialist Instructor
- Master Instructor
- Instructor Trainer
- Instructor Certifier

Technical / Extended Range Courses

- XR Nitrox Diver
- XR Limited Trimix Diver
- XR Advanced Wreck Diver
- XR Cavern Diver
- XR Technical Extended Range Diver
- XR Technical Extended Range Trimix Diver
- XR Hypoxic Trimix Diver
- XR Technical Wreck Diver
- XR Cave Diver
- XR Full Cave Diver
- XR Gas Blender

TDI/SDI - Technical Diving International / Scuba Diving International (www.tdisdi.com)

- Originated in 1994 as TDI with a focus on technical diving. SDI is a sister company which offers recreational courses. For ease of understanding, we have grouped them together in this manual.
- TDI says it offers the broadest range of technical courses available on the market.
- Active in over 100 countries
- Particularly known for their sport-level 'solo diver' course.

Recreational Courses

- Skin Diver
- Open Water SCUBA Diver
- Advanced Adventure Diver
- Rescue Diver
- Master SCUBA Diver Development Program

Specialty Courses

- Advanced Buoyancy
- Altitude Diver
- Boat Diver
- Computer Diver
- Computer Nitrox Diver
- CPROX Administrator Course
- CPR1st Administrator Course
- Deep Diver
- Diver Propulsion Vehicle
- Drift Diver
- Dry Suit Diver
- Equipment Specialist
- Full Face Mask Diver Specialty
- Ice Diver
- Marine Ecosystems Awareness
- Night- Limited Visibility Diver
- Research Diver
- Search and Recovery
- Shore/Beach Diver
- Sidemount Diver

- Solo Diver
- Underwater Hunter & Collector
- Underwater Navigation
- Underwater Photography
- Underwater Video
- Visual Inspection Procedures
- Wreck Diver

Professional Courses

- Divemaster Course
- Assistant Instructor Course
- Instructor Course
- Specialty Instructor
- IT Staff Instructor Qualifications
- Instructor Trainer Qualifications
- Online Instructor Crossover System (If you're currently an instructor with another organization, this is what allows you to crossover to SDI/TDI)

Technical Courses

- Intro to Tech Diving
- Nitrox Diver
- Advanced Nitrox Diver
- Decompression Procedures Diver
- Extended Range Diver
- Trimix Diver
- Advanced Trimix Diver
- Sidemount Diver
- Overhead Environment Courses
- Service Courses
- Cavern Diver
- Intro to Cave Diver
- Full Cave Diver
- Advanced Wreck Diver
- Cave DPV Diver
- Stage Cave Diver
- Cave Surveying Diver
- Semi-Closed Rebreather Diver
- Air Diluent Closed Circuit Rebreather Diver
- Basic Air Diluent Decompression Rebreather Diver
- Mixed Gas Closed Circuit Rebreather Diver

- Advanced Mix Gas Closed Circuit Rebreather Diver

CMAS - World Confederation of Underwater Activities (www.cmas.org)

- Not a training agency by itself but rather an international organization that recognizes local training federations. A complete list of these federations can be found here http://www.cmas.org/federation-list
- Though often locally very strongly represented and respected, an instructor certification from a federation in one country is often not immediately recognizable elsewhere.
- Members generally support a more militaristic approach to diver training

In the case of CMAS it's important to understand that they don't issue the certification but rather recognize the following levels, as issued by their member agencies.

Recreational Courses

- 1 Star Diver
- 2 Star Diver
- 3 Star Diver
- 4 Star Diver

Specialty Courses

- Apnoea Diver Level I
- Apnoea Diver Level II
- Apnoea Diver Level III
- Disabled Diver: Open Water Diving Environment Level I
- Disabled Diver: Open Water Diving Environment Level II
- Disabled Diver: Open Water Diving Environment Level III
- Enriched Air Nitrox Diver
- Drysuit Diver
- Altitude Diver
- Underwater Navigation
- Search and Recovery Diver
- Ice Diver
- Compressor Operator

- Nitrox Gas Blender
- Trimix Gas Blender
- Cave Diver Level I (Cavern Diver)
- Recreational Scooter Diver
- CPR & BLS
- Oxygen Administration
- Rescue Diver
- Recreational Trimix Diver
- Semi-Closed Rebreather Diver
- Advanced Semi-Closed Rebreather Diver
- Closed Circuit Rebreather Diver
- Children Diving Bronze Award
- Children Diving Gold Award
- Children Diving Silver Award
- Wreck Diver Level 1
- Wreck Diver Level 2

Professional Courses

- 1 Star Snorkel Instructor
- 2 Star Snorkel Instructor
- 1 Star Instructor
- 2 Star Instructor
- 3 Star Instructor

Technical Courses

- Advanced Nitrox Diver
- Advanced Semi-Closed Rebreather Diver
- Cave Diver Level II (Apprentice Cave Diver)
- Cave Diver Level III (Full Cave Diver)
- Extended Range Nitrox Diver
- Normoxic Trimix Diver
- Overhead environment Scooter
- Technical Scooter Diver
- Trimix Diver
- Advanced Trimix Diver

"Don't allow your mind to tell your heart what to do.
The mind gives up easily."

Paulo Coelho

DIVE SAGA

WWW.DIVESAGA.COM